As
yo

POT POURRI

Creating long-lasting natural fragrances for the home

POT POURRI

Creating long-lasting natural fragrances
for the home

JOANNA SHEEN

WARD LOCK

Also by Joanna Sheen
and published by Ward Lock:

Dried Flower Gardening
Herbal Gifts

I would like to dedicate this book to Jean as a thank you for her
pot pourri of ideas and inspirations, opinions and solutions that
she has given to all the family over the years

A WARD LOCK BOOK

First published in the UK 1992
by Ward Lock
(a Cassell imprint)
Villiers House
41/47 Strand
LONDON
WC2N 5JE

Distributed in the United States
by Sterling Publishing Co., Inc.
387 Park Avenue South, New York, NY 10016–8810

Distributed in Australia
by Capricorn Link (Australia) Pty Ltd
P.O. Box 665, Lane Cove, NSW 2066

British Library Cataloguing in Publication Data
Sheen, Joanna
   Pot pourri.
   I. Title
   745.92
   ISBN 0–7063–7014–7

Typeset by Columns Design and Production Services Ltd., Reading

Printed and bound in Hong Kong

Contents

Introduction

Mankind has been using natural perfumes and fragranced material for at least 6000 years. From the tombs of ancient Egypt to today's most modern interiors, gentle aromas (and some not so gentle!) have been used to make our living conditions more pleasant. Pot pourri is one of the most enduring and successful ways of scenting rooms, and the range of suitable ingredients means there is a pot pourri for every occasion.

I have covered many aspects of pot pourri in this book, from the traditional moist pot pourri to the more modern recipes for simmering pot pourri and fragranced pine cones. Whether you just want to dip into a book for ideas on home-made fragrant ideas, or intend to become really involved in making pot pourri, you will find many recipes and ideas that are new and unusual in this book. Drying flowers and herbs for use in pot pourri is a happy, relaxing pastime, and creating your own blend of pot pourri and other scented material is an addictive craft – so be warned!

While researching the historical details of pot pourri I came across this quotation which I loved:

'Also drye roses put to the nose to smell do comforte the braine and the harte and quencheth spirites –' Askham's Herbal, 1550

So, read on, and I hope that the fragrances you concoct will comfort your brain, heart and spirit!

Flowers, apple slices and cinnamon combine to create a special fragrance.

CHAPTER ONE

The History of Pot Pourri

Even several thousand years ago, the Egyptians were using perfumes, and the history of herbal and floral perfumes is well documented through the ages. Both the Greeks and the Romans used perfumes and incense for religious and domestic purposes. The heyday of roses, pot pourri and perfumes came in the seventeenth and eighteenth centuries, when all self-respecting housewives knew the good properties of herbs and flowers.

There are many books recording recipes carefully kept by several generations of a family, and which were passed down from mother to daughter. The art of fragrancing the linens, rooms in the house and clothing was considered an everyday task, in the same way as cooking or storing fruit by bottling and preserving it.

Many traditions are now being revived, and a bowl of sweet-smelling roses or pot pourri can gladden the heart as much today as it did in those earlier centuries.

Growing flowers in the garden and preserving them in a personal pot pourri mix is a lovely way to keep your summer memories.

Perfumes and incense played important parts in the everyday life of ancient Egyptians. They had many herbs and spices, resins and flowers that are still widely used today. Frankincense and myrrh, peppermint, cinnamon, juniper and sweet herbs were all common ingredients.

The Egyptian priests were skilled in mixing incense and perfume. Plutarch mentions a blend of herbs and resins known as Kyphi, saying that it 'lulled one to sleep, allayed anxieties, and brightened dreams'. The strength of this concoction obviously helped to bring on a state of ecstasy. This use of perfumes has been incorporated into the ceremonies of many religions; Hindus, Buddhists, Shintoists, Muslims and Christians all use incense, flowers or candles as part of their worship.

Although the priesthood tried in vain to keep the secrets of perfume as a religious phenomenon, it was soon taken up by anyone who could afford such luxury. Many famous people throughout history made great use of flowers, perfumes and scents. Cleopatra was particularly skilled in using cosmetics and perfumes; she made great use of oil distilled from lilies when she met Mark Antony and had the floor of the palace covered with a deep layer of rose petals.

World trade soon developed with the return of the Crusaders. They brought 'new' knowledge to Europe of exciting aromatics and perfumes. Many spices and resins were traded between such countries as India, China, Arabia, Persia and Assyria and Europe.

By the time Elizabeth I was on the throne in England, the techniques of distillation and perfumery in general were well established. In Elizabeth's court there were servants employed to keep up a good stock of herbs and flowers. Some staff were employed specifically to provide her with perfumes, pot pourris and delicacies such as lavender conserve. By now, every large house would have had a still-room, where the family recipes would be used to provide all the day-to-day needs of the household for perfumery, simple medications and cleaning materials. The still-room was a warm, dry room in which herbs and flowers were hung up to dry and oils were drawn from the flowers by distillation (hence the name, 'still-room').

Hygiene left a lot to be desired, so floors were strewn with sweet-smelling herbs to make them a less pleasant home for rodents, fleas and other uninvited guests, but much more comfortable for the human inhabitants of the house. Rosemary and lavender were very popular herbs, and old-fashioned roses were grown in many gardens. Most of the recipes from this period include roses in their list of ingredients – to eat, to drink and also to smell sweet.

In the past, the most popular way to use pot pourri was as a powder which was put into taffeta bags and stored between linen and clothing. It was also used, again in bags (known as 'sweet bags'), in the living areas, hung over chairs or placed on window sills to act as a natural air freshener. We worry about how our houses smell today but in comparison with these centuries gone by, we have little cause for concern. With little in the way of sewerage and rubbish disposal other than the easy way of burying things, the smell of the streets in a crowded town would have been quite something!

Another big difference between then and now concerns accepted washing habits. It would have been a very fussy man who ordered a bath to be drawn once a month – and probably a rich one at that. Many ordinary people only washed infrequently, and before the arrival of soap would rub oils into their skin and then scrape them off, taking the dirt with them. The mind boggles! At least the fragrant oils would have left the skin smelling sweet for a while! The old habit of wrapping up with goose grease through the winter must have added a special something to the smell in the house by the time spring arrived; the inhabitants would have been wrapped like that for some four or five months. The old saying 'Ne'er cast a clout till May is out', whether it refers to the month or the flowering bush matters not – people would still have worn those heavy winter clothes and grease for many months!

Traditional recipes were still used throughout the eighteenth and nineteenth centuries. With the discovery of the Americas, even more ingredients were included, such as allspice, vanilla and sassafras. By the end of the nineteenth century cosmetics were certainly here to stay, with a massive range of colognes, hair restoratives, pomades and other cosmetic items being manufactured all over the world. The advent of artificial perfumes made from chemical ingredients meant that the natural art of fragrance and pot pourri fell from favour during the early part of the twentieth century. But with the revival of country-based arts and crafts, we are turning once again to the traditional and natural ways of perfuming our bodies, our clothes and our homes.

EARLY RECIPES FOR POT POURRI

Earliest ways of making pot pourri centre around the moist method of manufacture. Originally called 'sweet jars', this method combines fresh petals and spices with large quantities of salt. The finished product is far stronger and longer lasting than a modern dry pot pourri but is best kept in a covered container as it looks very dull. The salt removes all the colour from the roses and other flowers and you are left with a very dead-looking collection of ingredients. The exact translation is 'rotten pot' – it certainly looks pretty rotten but it does smell divine!

Moist pot pourri produces such a strong-smelling mixture that some Victorian pot pourri jars that were left closed for decades still retained a faint aroma when they were eventually opened. I'm not suggesting that if you make your pot pourri in this way it will last indefinitely, but this really traditional method is certainly worth a try!

Many suitable containers are available from shops and you may even find some in your own cupboards. You should choose an attractive container that either has holes pierced in it or a removable lid. Alternatively, you could opt for a wooden box with a lattice-work or a porcelain jar with decorative holes pierced in the sides. The colours of the flowers used in the mixture are completely irrelevant as they will never be seen; the really important ingredient is fragrance.

Herbs take little maintenance and smell wonderful, whether fresh or dried, and are an important part of pot pourri manufacture.

Large rose hips make a welcome addition to autumnal colour in the garden and dry beautifully for pot pourri recipes.

A *sweet jar*

Here is a nineteenth-century recipe from the Countess of Rosse.

Four handfuls of Damask Roses
Four handfuls of Lavender flowers
Two handfuls of Orange flowers
Two handfuls of Clove Carnations
Also the flowers of Sweet Marjoram,
  Thyme, Rosemary, Myrtle and Mint
  of each one handful

One Seville orange stuck with cloves
  well dried and pounded
One ounce of Cinnamon
One ounce of Cloves
The rind of two lemons
Six Bay leaves

All the ingredients must be thoroughly dried but not in the sun. Mix them all together in a jar with bay salt.

Although this recipe is a little vague when it comes to the instructions and method, it is well worth using for its lovely selection of ingredients. Judging by another nineteenth-century recipe, I would suggest using between 8 oz (225 g or 1 cup) and 1 lb (450 g or 2 cups) of salt. Having dried all the ingredients well (see the section on air-drying in Chapter Two), arrange them in layers in a suitable container, with a layer of the flower mixture, followed by a layer of salt, and continuing until the pot is full. It can take several weeks for the mixture to mature but after two or three months it should be ready to be placed in an attractive container and displayed in one of the rooms in the house. This type of pot pourri is not meant to be constantly open to the air. Instead, you should remove the lid as you enter the room and replace it when you leave to conserve the precious perfume.

Many of the older recipes for moist pot pourri use ingredients which are difficult to obtain today. For example, the following recipe includes several unfamiliar ingredients, but the recipe works just as well when they are omitted. I increased the amount of calamus root to 1 lb (450 g or 2 cups) and omitted completely the rhodium wood and musk powder. The reference to damask rose leaves, confusingly enough, means rose petals not leaves!

Sweet scented bags to lay with linen

This recipe comes from Mrs Glasse, in her book *The Art of Cookery*, published in 1784. A drachm weighs $\frac{1}{16}$ oz (1.5 g).

Eight ounces of damask rose leaves	*Half an ounce of cloves*
Eight ounces of coriander seeds	*Four drachms of musk powder*
Eight ounces of Calamus aromaticus	*Two drachms of white loaf sugar*
One ounce Mace	*Three ounces Lavender flowers and*
One ounce cinnamon	*some Rhodium wood*

Beat them well together and make them in small silk bags.

There have been many suggestions over the years on how to cure sleeplessness. Hops are well known for their sleep-inducing qualities but here is a recipe from 1606 (Ram's *Little Deodon*) which uses roses. Whether it will help with sleeping problems I cannot say, but it smells lovely anyway! Perhaps if something soothing and sweet-smelling lies beside you on the pillow you are more likely to relax and thus sleep.

A Bag to Smell unto, or to Cause One to Sleep

Take drie Rose leaves, keep them close in a glasse which will keep them sweet, then take powder of Mints, powder of Cloves in a grosse powder. Put the same to the Rose leaves, then put all these together in a bag, and take that to bed with you, and it will cause you to sleep, and it is good to smell unto at other times.

A very rough translation of this recipe would be to take quantities of crumbled dried mint leaves, powdered cloves and dried rose petals and place them in a bag. You can alter amounts according to your own preference – I would suggest using a much smaller quantity of cloves than the other two ingredients as they can be somewhat overpowering.

OLD-FASHIONED INGREDIENTS AND THEIR MODERN ALTERNATIVES

Many ingredients that were in common usage in the past are either difficult to find or unacceptable to use today. Here is a list of these ingredients and where they originate from; if you want to follow some older pot pourri recipes you will at least recognize some of the more unusual ingredients.

Ambergris
This was used as a fixative and is a solid fatty substance expelled by sperm whales. It is often found floating on the sea or washed up on the shores of the Atlantic, the coasts of Africa, the East Indies, China and Japan. Ambergris is expensive and not easy to obtain now.

Musk
This is an oil extracted from the scent gland of the male musk deer, which is native to China, Nepal, Siberia and Tibet. For many years musk has been a very important ingredient in perfumery, but as the musk deer's existence is now threatened, the oil is usually synthesized.

Gum benzoin
This is referred to in old recipes as 'Benjamin'. It is a yellow resin produced by trees of the genus *Styrax*. A benzoin compound can sometimes be purchased from a pharmacy or from a specialist pot pourri supplier. Like ambergris, it is quite expensive.

MAKING SWEET WATER

A Book of Fruits and Flowers, published in 1653, gives an unusual recipe that produces some pot pourri and some sweet water at the same time.

To make a sweet cake, and with it a very sweet water
Take Damask Rose leaves, Bay leaves, Lavinder tops, sweet Marjerome tops, Ireos powder, Damask powder, and a little Musk first dissolved in sweet water, put the Rose leaves and herbs into a Bason, and sprinkle a quarter of a pint of Rose water among them, and stirring them all together, cover the Bason close with a dish, and let them stand so covered, all night, in the morning Distill them, so shall you have at once an excellent sweet water, and a very fine sweet Cake to lay among your finest linnen.

A modern method would be to mix all the ingredients as mentioned (you could add a little musk oil if you wished or simply omit it; Ireos powder is orris root) and leave them overnight as suggested. The next day you could leave the mixture to drain through a fine sieve until the petal mixture seems to be drying. The sweet water can then be bottled and used to perfume your washing water, added to the final rinse when washing your hair or sprinkled on to linens and lingerie. The petal mixture should be spread out to dry and can then be treated like a moist pot pourri; in other words, smelt but not seen!

OTHER TRADITIONAL RECIPES

Many of the traditional recipes can be inspirational, and a recipe that springs to mind is from *The Queen's Closet Opened*, a trilogy of useful books about culinary, medical and confectionery matters first published in 1655.

King Edward's perfume
Take twelve spoonfuls of right red Rosewater, the weight of six pence in fine powder of Sugar, and boil it on hot embers and coles softly, and the house will smell as though it were full of Roses; but you must burn the sweet Cypress wood before to take away the gross air.

SIMMERING POT POURRI

Chapter Six in this book deals with simmering pot pourri which, although not a new concept, is less well-known in some countries than the dry pot pourri. There is, however, a recipe dating back to 1662 published in a book called *A Queen's Delight* for a very early simmering pot pourri.

An odoriferous parfume for chambers
Take a glasseful of Rose Water, Cloves well beaten to powder, a penny weight: then take the fire panne and make it red hot in the fyre, and put thereon of the said Rose water with the sayd pouder of Cloves making it so consume, by little and little but the rose water must be muskt, and you shall make a parfume of excellent good odour.

A rough translation would be to add a tablespoon (15 g) of cloves to half a pint (300 ml) of rose water. In a saucepan, add a drop or two of musk oil to the rose water and then put it on a medium heat; the resulting perfume will fill the air with a lovely smell that is subtle but very addictive. I have made this recipe several times, but always omit the musk oil and add other essential oils instead – it smells heavenly.

You can easily buy rose water, but it is always interesting to make your own. This recipe comes from another very old book – *The Whole Body of Cookery Dissected* by William Rabisha, published in 1675. Many of the recipes seem very complicated but this is amazingly simple and it works!

Musk rose water
Take two handfuls of your Musk Rose leaves, put them into about a quart of fair water and a quarter of a pound of sugar, let this stand and steep for about half an hour, then take your water and flowers and pour them out of one vessel into another till such time as the water hath taken the scent and taste of the flowers, then set it in a cool place a-cooling and you will find it a most excellent scent water.

MOIST POT POURRI

Enough of the original and elderly recipes! Having spent some time researching the old ways to make pot pourri and other fragrant things, it becomes easier to create new recipes for moist pot pourri, for example, using modern and easily obtainable ingredients.

Although I give the measurements in cups, any container will do, as long as you keep to the correct proportions – don't alter your measuring jug or cup halfway through a recipe!

If your pot pourri becomes too wet, you can dry it out by adding some more orris root. If the mixture becomes completely dry, try adding some more salt. Ideally, the mixture should be moist in order to work most effectively.

Victorian pot pourri

8 cups scented rose petals, preferably dark red
2 cups lavender flowers
2 cups rose-scented geranium leaves
8 bay leaves
1½ cups sea salt
½ cup mixed allspice, cloves and crushed cinnamon
½ cup brown sugar
½ cup cheap brandy
½ cup powdered orris root

Take two large bowls, and in one bowl mix the rose petals, geranium leaves and lavender flowers with the orris powder. In the other bowl, mix together all the remaining ingredients except the brandy. Choose a large container with a lid in which to mature the pot pourri and arrange the mixtures in layers, beginning with a rose petal layer followed by a salt mixture layer, until you have exhausted all your ingredients. Then pour the brandy gently over the top and weigh the mixture down with a plate and a heavy weight from a set of scales, a flat iron or anything else that is reasonably heavy. Replace the lid on the container.

This mixture will be mature after between 4–6 weeks but should be stirred every day. After about 5 weeks have passed, check the fragrance; if necessary you can add more spices or, if the flower scent is too weak, you can cheat and add some drops of the relevant essential oils. Once you are happy with the scent, you can decant the mixture into a pot pourri container that has a wide neck and a lid. Do not keep the lid off all the time, but just remove it occasionally to perfume the room.

Whenever the mixture needs reviving try giving it a good stir. When this no longer works, you can add some more brandy and a little more salt.

Many ingredients are suitable for moist pot pourri but these are some of the more popular choices. Although moist pot pourri takes a little longer to make, the fragrance is extremely long lasting.

EXPERIMENTING WITH INGREDIENTS

Most recipes for moist pot pourri include rose petals as a base, and these are no exception, but it might be worth experimenting with other aromatic flowers and leaves from time to time. The enjoyable thing about making your own pot pourri is that you can use whatever you want. You are the designer, the creator, and apart from following some basic guidelines on the actual process you can alter recipes as much as you like. The main drawback with moist pot pourri is its appearance. This can easily be camouflaged by decorating the top of a container with roses and other flowers individually dried in silica gel, as shown in the photographs. So experiment with both kinds of pot pourri making and decide which sort you prefer – I'm going to sit on the fence and say that I like them both for different reasons.

Spring fever

As many recipes call for rose petals, it might seem that making moist pot pourri is mainly a task for high summer, but that is not so. This is a gorgeous spring pot pourri with a wonderfully subtle fragrance that would be impossible to reproduce with chemical or synthetic smells.

8 cups hyacinth florets
2 cups freesia flowers
2 cups narcissus flowers, 'Cheerfulness'
  are good
2 cups prunus or cherry blossom
1½ cups sea salt
½ cup cheap brandy

½ cup mixed spices, such as nutmeg,
  cloves and allspice
½ cup powdered orris root
juice of one orange and its chopped peel
optional – few drops neroli (orange
  blossom) essential oil

Mix together the salt, spices, orange peel and juice with the orris root. In a separate container mix together all the flowers. Then in a large pot with a tight-fitting lid, arrange alternate layers of the flowers and salt mixtures, and pour the brandy over the top. Weigh the mixture down with a plate and a heavy weight, and replace the lid. Stir once a day or so for between 4–6 weeks. Once the mixture has matured you can check it for strength of smell. If you feel it needs to be a little stronger, add a few drops of neroli oil or another to suit your taste.

Many other possibilities will occur to you when you begin to search your garden for fragrant ideas. One combination I am longing to try once I have grown the necessary flowers is a naturally chocolate-scented pot pourri. *Cosmos atrosanguineus* smells of chocolate, as does *Pittosporum tenuifolium* and also, I believe, *Corokia* x *virgata*. Perhaps if you made a mixture of chocolate-smelling flowers and mint leaves, brandy and a little orange, you could call it after-dinner pot pourri?

Roses in the kitchen
This recipe uses mainly culinary herbs with the roses, hence the name.

8 cups scented rose petals
1 cup mint leaves
1 cup sprays of thyme leaves
1 cup rosemary leaves
1 cup pot marjoram flowers
1 cup knotted oregano

1 cup crumbled bay leaves
2 cups sea salt
1 cup mixed spices of your choice
1 cup powdered orris root
¾ cup brandy
¼ cup lemon juice

Mix together all the ingredients except the salt, brandy and lemon juice. Arrange in layers in a container with a tight-fitting lid, starting with a layer of rose mixture, then covering that with a layer of salt, and so on. When all the ingredients are used up, pour the brandy and lemon juice over the top of them. Cover the top with a plate, held in place with a heavy weight, and replace the lid. Leave within easy reach as you need to stir the mixture every day. After about 6 weeks it will be matured. You can then put it into suitable containers to perfume the house. Additional decorations can be added to the top of the pot pourri such as whole flowers and spices, if you use containers that are not sealed.

Plum, cloves and cinnamon
This recipe has a lovely smell of cloves, so avoid it if you are not overkeen on their scent. Although made up in high summer, this is a lovely pot pourri to use at Christmas time when the smell of cloves blends well with other seasonal scents.

4 cups peony petals
4 cups damask rose petals
2 cups mixed carnations and pinks
2 cups Sweet William flowers
2 cups stock flowers
2 cups Iris graminea flowers (they
  smell of stewed plums)

2 cups sea salt
½ cup cloves
½ cup crushed cinnamon sticks
½ cup powdered orris root
½ cup brandy with a little lemon
  juice
chopped peel of two lemons

Mix the sea salt with the spices, orris root and lemon peel. In another container mix together all the flower heads. Fill a large container, with a lid, with the mixture. Start with a layer of flower heads then sprinkle some salt mixture over them, and continue in this way until you have used up all the ingredients. Then pour the brandy and lemon juice over the top of the mixture and weigh it down with a plate and a heavy weight. Stir every day for about 4–6 weeks, by which time the pot pourri should have matured. If you are not happy with the smell you can cheat and add some drops of essential oil to alter the balance of the fragrance or its intensity. A possible choice for this pot pourri recipe might be essential oil of roses or, as that is usually a very expensive option, perhaps oil of sweet orange. If the clove smell is not already quite strong you could add some oil of cloves.

CHAPTER TWO

Collecting your Ingredients

Many of the ingredients needed for pot pourri are available from easy-to-reach sources, such as your own back garden, the supermarket and possibly a pharmacy or florist. There are also specialist sources mentioned at the back of the book for unusual pot pourri supplies. In this chapter there are clear descriptions of many potential ingredients and how to use them, plus whether to grow them or buy them. There is also a section on essential oils, which I would always recommend buying rather than attempting to make yourself.

Although the mixtures you create can be your own, it is always useful to be able to refer back to ideas for basic ingredients, their colours, sizes and shapes before you begin creating yourself!

Roses make a beautiful addition to the garden and are very useful as the basic ingredient for many pot pourri mixes.

The first and most important ingredient of pot pourri is usually scented flower petals. Of course, there are occasions when this is not the case, and a recipe uses only scented cones and mosses or berries, for example, but flowers are the most common ingredients. It is important, therefore, to have a good supply of the necessary flowers for the particular recipe that you wish to follow.

The main ingredients in a great many recipes are rose petals. However, it is important to have the right sort of roses, and the best way to obtain these is to grow them in your garden. You can buy hybrid tea roses with petals in many lovely colours, but it is unlikely that they will have any smell at all. If you wish to use hybrid tea or floribunda roses because you already grow them, you can add the necessary fragrance with an essential rose oil.

The ideal ingredients, however, are the old-fashioned Rosa Mundi, Apothecary's Rose (*Rosa officinalis*), cabbage roses, damask roses and the most highly scented of the bourbon roses, such as 'Parfum de l'Hay' and 'George Dickson'. The rugosa and centifolia hybrids are also good. All of these should be easily available from specialist rose growers.

ESSENTIAL OILS

Apart from the old-fashioned roses, there are many other herbal plants that have distinct fragrances, but none are strong enough to perfume a room for long. If you are making the dry type of pot pourri (the methods and recipes for this are in Chapter Four), then you will probably have to rely on essential oils and perfume oils.

An essential oil is extracted from the actual flower or plant and is a single pure scent. A perfume oil is usually a combination of scents, which may or may not contain essential oils and chemically synthesized scents. That is not to say that the essential oils are superior – if you want a particular perfume it may only be available in a ready-mixed perfume oil. It is usually cheaper to buy a mixed oil that you really like rather than to buy a whole selection of essential oils and try to copy your favourite perfume.

However, if you want to create something new, different and exciting, the individual essential oils are like a painter's palette and will provide you with endless choices and wonderful scope for experimentation. One word of warning, though; they are very strong and once the pot pourri has matured its smell is not always what you expected. So make small quantities at a time in case you don't like the result, and always keep careful notes when you make up a new recipe.

For the brave, or those who insist on keeping strictly to tradition, here are a couple of methods for extracting your own essential oils. But don't forget that I recommend buying them rather than making them yourself!

Oyle of Roses
This first method comes from the *Book of Fruits and Flowers*, first published in 1653, and suggests the following.

Take Sallet Oyle and put it into an earthen pot, then take Rose leaves, clip off all the white, and bruise them a little, and put them into the Oyle, and then stop the top close with paste, and set it into a boyling pot of water, and let it boyle one hour, then let it stand al one night upon hot embers, the next day take the Oyle, and straine it from the Rose leaves, into a glasse, and put therein some fresh Rose leaves, clipt as before, stop it, and set it in the Sun every day for a fortnight or three weeks.

Essential oil from roses

This is a more modern recipe.

Take a quantity of plain vegetable oil (I would suggest grapeseed or sunflower) and immerse in the oil as many rose petals as you can cram until they are no longer covered by the oil. Leave the petals to soak in the oil and stir well every six to eight hours for two days.

After two days, remove the first batch of rose petals and add a second one, soaking them for two days and stirring regularly. Continue to replace the rose petals every couple of days for at least another ten days or more, depending on the strength of perfume obtained. The oil still won't be as strong as a commercially produced oil or attar of roses, but you will have some satisfaction in knowing that you made it yourself! You should, by the way, use scented rose petals and not the commercial varieties that have very little or no perfume.

SUITABLE FLOWERS FOR POT POURRI

Bearing in mind that the major roles played by the flowers are those of decoration and bulk, then there are many different varieties to recommend. All flowers will dry, after a fashion, but the important thing is to pick those varieties that will give a good shape and a good colour; if they have a fragrance that can be a bonus.

The easiest way to catalogue possible flowers is probably by listing them alphabetically under their Latin names, to ensure that we are all talking about the same plant – common plant names can vary from place to place.

Flowers that bloom during the winter/spring

NAME	COLOUR	METHOD
Abutilon suntense	Blue	Silica
Acacia dealbata (Mimosa)	Yellow	Air-dry or press
Aquilegia alpina	Blue	Silica or press
Clematis armandii	White	Silica
Clematis armandii 'Apple Blossom'	Pink	Silica
Clematis montana 'Elizabeth'	Pink	Silica
Erica herbacea (Heather)	White	Air-dry or glycerine
Erica praecox 'Rubra'	Pink	Silica
Erythronium revolutum (Dog tooth violet)	White	Silica or press

Galanthus nivalis (Snowdrop)	White	Silica or press
Helleborus atrorubens	Pink	Silica or press
Helleborus orientalis	White	Silica or press
Iris uniquicularis 'Alba'	White	Silica
Jasminum officinale	White	Silica or press
Kerria japonica (Jew's mallow)	Yellow	Silica or press
Lonicera fragrantissima (Honeysuckle)	White	Silica or press
Narcissus jonquilla	Yellow	Silica
Narcissus 'Paper White'	White	Silica
Paeonia lactiflora	White	Air-dry or silica
Primula vulgaris (Primrose)	Yellow	Silica or press
Prunus 'Accolade' (Flowering cherry)	Pink	Silica
Prunus 'Tai Haku' (Flowering cherry)	White	Silica
Tulipa 'Monte Carlo'	Yellow	Silica
Vinca minor (Periwinkle)	Blue	Silica
Viola 'Mount Everest'	White	Silica or press
Viola odorata	Blue	Silica or press
Viola wittrockiana 'Azure Blue'	Blue	Silica or press

Lavender plays an important part in many pot pourri recipes and is a beautiful plant to grow in the garden.

24

Pansies are amongst the easiest plants to have in the garden and they look so pretty when they are preserved in silica crystals or pressed.

Flowers that bloom early to late summer

NAME	COLOUR	METHOD
Achillea 'Moonshine'	Yellow	Air-dry
Achillea ptarmica	White	Air-dry
Alchemilla mollis (Lady's mantle)	Yellow	Air-dry
Anemone sp. (Windflower)	White	Silica or press
Anemone fulgens	Red	Silica or press
Anemone 'Prinz Heinrich'	Pink	Silica or press
Anthemis cupiana	White	Silica or press
Anthemis tinctoria	Yellow	Silica or press
Astrantia major	White	Silica or press
Centaurea dealbata	Pink	Silica or air-dry
Clematis tangutica	Yellow	Silica or glycerine
Convallaria majalis (Lily of the valley)	White	Silica
Cosmos atrosanguineus	Red	Silica or press
Delphinium 'Blue Dawn'	Blue	Air-dry or silica
Dianthus sp. (Carnations and pinks)	Red	Air-dry or silica
Dianthus 'Doris'	Pink	Air-dry or silica
Dianthus 'Mrs Sinkins'	White	Air-dry or silica
Echinops ritro	Blue	Air-dry
Eryngium giganticum	Blue	Air-dry
Fuchsia magellanica	Pink	Silica or press
Geum 'Mrs Bradshaw'	Red	Silica or press
Heuchera sanguinea	Pink	Press

Hydrangea arborescens	White	Air-dry or press
Hydrangea macrophylla	Blue	Air-dry or press
Hydrangea macrophylla	Pink	Air-dry or press
Lavandula angustifolium (Lavender)	Blue	Air-dry
Lilium regale	White	Silica
Nigella damascena	Blue	Silica or press
Nymphaea odorata sulphurea (Water lily)	Yellow	Silica or press
Paeonia officinalis	Pink	Air-dry or silica
Paeonia peregrince	Red	Air-dry or silica
Philadelphus coronarius (Mock orange)	White	Silica or press
Potentilla 'Elizabeth'	Yellow	Silica or press
Potentilla 'Miss Willmott'	Red	Silica or press
Rosa 'Canary Bird'	Yellow	Silica or press
Rosa 'Constance Spry'	Pink	Silica or air-dry
Rosa 'Ispahan' (damask)	Pink	Silica or air-dry
Rosa 'Mme Pierre Oger' (bourbon)	Pink	Silica or air-dry
Rosa rugosa 'Blanc Double de Coubert'	White	Silica or air-dry
Tagetes patula (French marigold)	Yellow	Silica
Thymus serpyllum	Pink	Air-dry or press
Tricyrtis formosana (Toad lily)	Red	Silica
Viola wittrockiana 'Arkwright Ruby'	Red	Silica or press

HERBS AND LEAVES FOR POT POURRI

Many different kinds of herb blend beautifully in pot pourri and leaves also make a good colourful display and add bulk to the mixture. In theory, everything will dry, but some varieties dry better than others and have colour or scent in their favour. I have listed them all under their Latin names as I feel that is a better worldwide reference than their common names.

It is best to use small leaves and sprays of herbal plants; if you use large leaves the mixture can look very messy and untidy. The one exception to that rule concerns an autumn leaf collection which, when mixed with acorns and nuts, could look very interesting. As a general rule of thumb, however, I would suggest using small to medium-sized pieces of herb and leaf, and letting the flowers star in your mixtures.

Herbs
Allium schoenoprasum (Chives) Pink flower heads
Aloysia triphylla (Lemon verbena) Scented leaves
Anethum graveolens (Dill) Yellow flowers
Angelica archangelica (Angelica) Leaves and roots
Artemisia Silver leaves
Borago officinalis (Borage) Dainty blue flowers
Cedronella canariensis (Balm of Gilead) Scented leaves
Chamaemelum nobile (Camomile) Flowers and leaves

Coriandrum sativum (Coriander) Seeds
Foeniculum vulgare (Fennel) Yellow flowers
Hesperis matronalis (Sweet rocket) Pink flowers
Humulus lupulus (Hops) Dried green flowers
Hyssopus officinalis (Hyssop) Pink/mauve flowers and leaves
Laurus nobilis (Sweet bay) Leaves
Mentha species (Mints) Leaves and flowers
Melissa officinalis (Lemon balm) Leaves
Monarda didyma (Bergamot) Red flowers and leaves
Myrtus communis (Myrtle) Flowers and leaves
Origanum species (Marjoram and oregano) Leaves and flowers
Pelargonium species (Scented geraniums) Leaves
Rosmarinus officinalis (Rosemary) Leaves, stems and flowers
Santolina chamaecyparissus (Santolina) Leaves and flowers
Salvia officinalis (Sage) Leaves
Thymus sp. (Thyme) Leaves and flowers

These herbs can all be dried using one of the air-drying methods described in Chapter Four. You can dry them in silica gel if you want a better result but as they are usually crushed into the bulk of the mixture it is not worth the time and effort. If, however, you want to make a special herb mixture and need some perfect specimens to decorate the top of it, then silica gel would be ideal for drying them.

Leaves

Any leaf can be air-dried and then crumbled to add to the bulk of pot pourri, but it is better to choose a leaf for a particular reason, such as the scent, colour, shape or texture. Bulking-out ingredients are always useful but should be used with caution as you can very easily end up with a pot pourri that looks dull and uninteresting. All the ingredients should be included for a purpose and should contribute something positive to the recipe. I have listed here a small selection of leaves that might be useful.

Acaena magellanica (New Zealand burr) Blue/grey leaves
Ajuga reptans (Bugle) Variegated or purple bronze
Berberis thunbergii Red/purple
Cotinus coggygria (Smoke bush) Purple
Cotoneaster horizontalis Variegated and turns pink
Eucalyptus gunnii Blue/grey
Fragaria vesca (Alpine strawberry) Variegated or green
Hebe andersonii Variegated
Hedera helix (Ivy) Variegated and also golden forms
Ligustrum ovalifolium (Golden privet) Golden
Pittosporum tenuifolium Variegated
Rosa rubrifolia (Rose) Pink/green
Ruta graveolens (Rue) Blue/grey

BOUGAINVILLEA

ALDER

ROSEMARY

CHILLIES

ROSEBUDS

NUTMEGS

PINGUATICA LEAVES

LARCH CONES

PINAS CONES

TULIPS

CYPRESS CONES

POPPY PETALS

STAR ANISE

CINNAMON STICKS

SITKA CONES

PINK GLOBE AMARANTH

CACTUS FLOWERS

MARIGOLDS

ROOT GINGER PEELED

LEMON GRASS

PEACH STONE

ROSE HIPS

APPLE SLICES

CITRUS PEELS, WOODS, CONES AND SPICES

This group of ingredients is very important as many of them add significantly to the fragrance of your pot pourri. The cones add a lovely texture and many of these ingredients can be found in your store cupboard, local woods or, in the case of the spices, bought in a nearby health food store.

Citrus peels

Orange, tangerine, lemon, lime and grapefruit can all be peeled thinly and then the resulting spirals of peel left to dry naturally in a warm place. Alternatively, the peel can be chopped before it is dried to speed up the drying process.

Berries

Juniper berries, rose hips, hawthorn berries and elder berries.

Woods

Cedar wood chips or shavings, quassia chips, cinnamon bark, ginger root and sandalwood chips.

Cones

Pine, alder, larch, costus flowers (which look like small cones), beech husks and acorns.

Spices

Allspice berries, cardamom seeds, chillies, cloves, nutmeg and mace, vanilla pods, coriander, cumin seeds and star anise.

All the above ingredients can be left in a warm place to dry naturally.

Selection of dried ingredients.

UNUSUAL INGREDIENTS

The only thing limiting the number of ingredients that you may use in your pot pourri making is your imagination. When thinking of new ideas for pot pourri look around you with an open mind.

The sea shore can be a veritable treasure trove. Small pieces of driftwood can be included, with or without a little essential oil dropped on to them. The small pieces of glass that the sea turns into beautiful rounded pebbles can be soaked in essential oil and used as decorations. Shells are a beautiful addition, especially for a mixture with a blue theme, as it looks very attractive to have little pearly shells nestling among the flowers.

Large shells can, of course, be used as containers for pot pourri, either left plain or decorated with dried flowers. To do this, use a strong glue or a hot-glue gun to stick silica dried flowers around the edge of the shell. This gives a lovely soft edge to the container.

Seaweed can also be incorporated into the recipe. Rinse the seaweed very thoroughly indeed after you have collected it and lay it out to dry on a wad of newspaper. The colours vary and can sometimes be rather dull but there are some interesting reds and greens to be found as well as the boring browns.

Still on the seashore, unusual finds such as a sea anemone shell, a seahorse or starfish can make a pretty decoration for a pot pourri with a marine theme! You could also include small clear or pale blue and green marbles to represent air bubbles. There are always lovely stones and pebbles on the beach and although it's a little difficult to perfume them with essential oils (you can try soaking them for a while), they can add a pretty finishing touch to an unusual collection of bits and pieces.

Apart from the citrus peels which are very popular ingredients, you can also use several other fruits in your recipes. Apple slices, especially when they are impregnated with cinnamon oil, look and smell wonderful. These are made by taking a rosy red apple and slicing it fairly thinly (¼ inch [6 mm] thick at the most) right across the core. Then lay these slices flat on a baking sheet and place in the lowest possible oven to dry out in the same way as you would meringues. I usually leave them overnight. You could use green apples, but they don't seem to keep their colour and turn a yellow brown instead, so the darker red apples are by far the most effective. Mango peel can be dried in the same way, as can pear and melon skins.

Kumquats can be dried whole, nuts of all varieties can be added for effect and cereals such as wheat, barley and oats can also go into the mix. Most botanical items are suitable if they give the effect that you want. A spring pot pourri would look very attractive with a sprinkling of pussy willow on the top.

Another possible hunting ground would be an old box of junk jewellery. Broken pearls, wooden or glass beads and gold and silver bits and bobs can add another dimension to your display. At Christmas it looks very effective to create a pot pourri with gold beads and shapes included in the mix, and you can also spray some botanical items with gold paint to add to the festive glitter.

FIXATIVES AND SCENTED BLENDERS

Many writers on pot pourri describe a large number of items as fixatives – substances added to the mix that will fix or hold the main scent. However, many additives are often recommended as first-class fixatives when they should really be described as second-class fixatives. I have divided the possible additions to your recipes into the categories of strong fixatives and weaker ones.

The main function of a fixative is to absorb the essential oils and perfumes of a recipe, and it need not have any scent of its own to contribute. The weaker fixatives usually do have a scent of their own and can also absorb some of the essential oils used, thereby acting as excellent blending ingredients. Many popular fixatives are used in a powdered form, which is excellent for moist pot pourri as it will be smelt but not seen. The powder is also useful when making sachets and other hidden scented ideas. If your mixture is to be displayed and needs to look as beautiful as possible, it is far better to use the cut form of such items as orris root or cellulose.

Weaker blending fixatives

Animal products, such as ambergris (from a sperm whale), castorium (from a beaver), civet (from a civet cat) and musk (from the musk deer) all come into this category. In my opinion, however, all these products in their original state (in other words the real version rather than a chemically synthesized one) should be completely ignored. There are hundreds of lovely botanical ingredients to experiment with, and the last thing we need to do is use animal products.

Gum resins, such as myrrh, frankincense, gum arabic, benzoin and storax are all excellent when added to any recipe as they bring all the smells and ingredients together and help to blend the perfumes. They do not, however, hold the perfume in the same way as the first-class fixatives.

Roots and seeds such as angelica root, vanilla pods, tonka beans, coriander, vetiver root, hibiscus and spices in general are all good for blending but not strong enough to fix the main scent.

First-class fixatives

The main fixatives that I have had real success with are limited in range but completely trustworthy.

The root of *Iris florentina* is more commonly known as orris root and, in both its cut and powdered forms, provides a really good fixative that you can rely upon. Equally reliable is the root of *Acorus calamus*, and oakmoss also

It is useful to build up a collection of different oils and fixatives which can easily be stored in glass screwtop containers.

works well. Orris and calamus roots are available from a pot pourri supplier (see the back of the book for details). Oakmoss is fairly easy to find in the wild or can also be bought from pot pourri suppliers.

Another fixative that works really well is cellulose. Corn cobs can be processed commercially to produce a substance that looks almost indistinguishable from the real cut orris root and has an added bonus (apart from its lower price) that it cannot produce an allergic reaction, unlike orris root. I am currently experimenting with other roots but cannot yet be sure of their long-lasting properties. Other possibilities are rhubarb root, sarsparilla root, wild yam root and angelica root, all of which are only available from specialist suppliers, but are nevertheless worth experimenting with.

THE DIFFERENT ESSENTIAL OILS

There are several groups into which you can divide the aromas you will use in creating a perfume. It is usually preferable to build up the fragrance by using other oils from the same aromatic group rather than adding completely unrelated smells which can virtually cancel each other out.

The categories can be listed as follows.

Animal or sensual and spicy
This is the strongest smelling group of natural fragrances. Only very small amounts are usually needed as these fragrances can easily become overpowering. The oils include musk, one of the most popular perfume oils, and which is taken from the scent gland of a male musk deer. Happily a synthetic musk is available, so if this is the section of perfume that appeals to you, there is no need to use animal products. Also included in this section are ambergris, civet and castorium, which are all also available in synthetic form.

The scents in this section are heavy and sweet and the plant extract oils include patchouli, vanilla, cinnamon, nutmeg and bitter almond.

Citrus and fruity
Apart from the obvious citrus fruit peels, there are many herbs that come into this section and oils are available in many of the well-known fragrances. Lemon grass, lemon verbena, lemon balm, bergamot and sweet orange are all available as natural oils. Many synthetic oils can be used from this section too, to make fresh and invigorating perfumes. Strawberry and peach scented pot pourri have been world favourites for some time, but less usual oils such as pear (delicious with ginger) and coconut can lead you down an interesting trail!

Floral
This is the traditional section and also, I must confess, my absolute favourite. I think there is nothing to beat the smell of old-fashioned roses,

lavender or jasmine. This is the section that produces the more relaxing, gentle and even narcotic scents.

Many natural and synthetic oils are available with floral fragrances, such as violet, hyacinth, lily of the valley, carnation, rose and honeysuckle to name but a few. Floral scents can also be mixed with either citrus or sensual fragrances from the previous two groups.

Mints, herbs and menthol

These are fresh, invigorating smells that can be quite sharp or mixed with another oil to tone them down. The basic group includes, eucalyptus, cedar wood, peppermint, fennel, cypress, camphor and pine.

This group is ideal for creating a fresh outdoor type of scent that would blend well with a sharp fruity smell such as lemon or lime. These scents can also work well with Christmas smells such as cinnamon and mulled wine.

All these oils and many more are available as single fragrances and as synthetic perfume oils. Try to smell every oil you come across and, if it appeals, gradually build up your collection. It doesn't take long to develop a fairly long row of little bottles which can be the start of a whole new interest for you and your friends.

CHAPTER THREE

Drying and Preserving your Flowers, Herbs and Leaves

Many pot pourri ingredients can be bought from specialist suppliers, and sometimes even from local supermarkets and health food stores. However, really keen recruits will want to preserve many of the plants from their gardens and possibly grow some, especially for pot pourri work.

The bulk of material in pot pourri can be dried quickly, because it will not be seen as an individual item. The flowers to decorate the top of the pot pourri, however, should be as beautiful as possible. This calls for drying with silica gel because the results, as well as being startlingly beautiful sometimes, are of a much higher standard than that achieved with air-drying.

None of the methods described in this chapter are complicated. The silica gel crystals have to be handled with a little patience, but the end result and the satisfaction to be obtained from growing and drying your own material is well worth all the effort involved.

Your garden can be an Aladdin's cave of potential ingredients, and the fruits of a walk through the woods can always be put to good use.

Apart from the many flowers and herbs mentioned in the previous chapter, there are probably plenty of others in your garden that you would like to try to preserve. All flowers and plant material can be dried – what we are concerned with is how they look once that process has taken place. Some plant material looks much better dried than others.

AIR-DRYING

Most leaves are much tougher than flowers and don't need quite such gentle handling. In the case of herbs and sprigs of leaves or individual leaves, they are best air-dried. This can be accomplished in a number of ways, depending on the time at your disposal and the space you have available.

Hanging up bunches to air-dry

If you have harvested large amounts of herbs or sprays of leaves then they can be tied in bunches and hung from a hook or beam in a dark corner of a room. They need good air circulation, no sunlight and an evenly warm temperature. Do not make your bunches too large or the plant material in the middle of the bunch will take much much longer to dry than that on the outside. In extreme cases, it may turn brown and nasty before it ever dries.

Tie your bunches with an elastic band. This is essential, because plant stems shrink during the drying process, and if you use string or some other material that does not shrink with the stems then you will have a heap of leaves or herbs lying on the floor after a few days! If you can spare the space in an airing cupboard, it makes a very efficient place for air-drying, provided there are good ventilation holes so the air can circulate.

It is advisable to keep your bunches to one variety only, since a mixed bunch may include an ingredient that dries far slower than the rest of the plant material and may cause problems. Once hung in a warm airy position, the bunches will take from about a week to four weeks to dry, depending on the contents and size of the bunch and the ambient temperature and humidity around it.

Air-drying – the flat method

Many plant pieces harvested for use in a pot pourri mix are too small to be bunched or hung up, so you need an alternative method for dealing with these items. Herb plants are often not large enough to cut bunches from and the trimmings are only 2 or 3 in (5 or 7.5 cm) long.

The best way to air-dry small pieces of foliage is to make up some rectangular frames. The outer edges are made from offcuts of wood or dowelling, and should measure something in the region of 24 × 18 in (60 × 45 cm). Having made the outer framework you should attach a piece of fine wire mesh (similar to the type that you would find on a sieve) by tacking it around the underside of the frame. You now have a rough and ready rectangular sieve. I have fixed some small blocks of wood to the corners of mine to make small feet so that the air can circulate all round the plant material.

The plant material is then laid on to the wire mesh, with no two pieces touching, and the sieve placed in a warm, dry and shady place. Depending on the temperature and the type of material you are drying, it may well be dry within a week.

For those of you who cannot wait a week for something to dry, there are a couple of possible short-cuts.

Drying in the microwave oven

As all this plant material is to be broken up and used as bulk in pot pourri, the finished shape is not overly important. It is possible therefore to dry small pieces of foliage or herbs directly in a microwave oven. Place a layer of absorbent kitchen paper on the turntable or base of the microwave and lay a few pieces of foliage inside. Cook on a medium heat for about two minutes and then check to see if it is quite dry. If it still seems to be a little damp then cook for a further twenty to thirty seconds and check it again.

If you do not want to use a microwave, it is also easy to dry this type of material in a conventional gas or electric oven.

Drying in a conventional oven

If you are using an electric oven, then set the thermostat as low as possible and place the foliage on a clean baking sheet. Put the baking sheet at the bottom of the oven and bake until all the foliage is dry. Keep a constant eye on it and remove each piece once it is dry. The Sunday roast never tastes the same with miscellaneous pieces of pot pourri foliage scenting the oven, which is what usually happens if I leave the plant material in the oven, because I forget all about it!

If you have a gas oven, warm it up by running it at the lowest temperature possible for about five minutes. Then turn off the gas and place the baking sheet in the oven. Keep a careful eye on it and remove it once all the foliage has dried. You should never place plant material in a gas oven that is alight because that would constitute a fire hazard and, quite apart from ruining your oven, it would also overcook the foliage!

If you want to keep their colour well, and don't want to invest in silica gel crystals, then pressing some of your flowers may be the answer.

PRESSING FLOWERS

The main drawback to preserving your flowers by pressing them is that they are reduced to two dimensions instead of three – in other words, they are flattened. Even so, they still look very effective when placed on top of a pot pourri mixture and can really come into their own if you want to display your pot pourri in a glass jar or container. By using glass you can decorate the sides of the pot pourri mix as well as the top. Using a small palette knife you can slide pressed flowers down the sides of the jar after you have filled it with the bulk of the pot pourri mixture. Then you can put either pressed or preserved flowers on the top to finish it off.

Many of the flowers listed in the previous chapters can be pressed, and it is a very straightforward and simple process. The main piece of equipment that you will need is a flower press. The traditional type sold in children's toy shops and craft stores is perfectly adequate. Alternatively, you can ask a handy friend or relative to make one for you.

Picking the flowers
It is more crucial when pressing flowers, rather than air-drying them, to pick them at the right time of day. Ideally, there should have been no rain for 24 hours and it should be a bright sunny day. Pick your flowers about mid-morning, when the dew has evaporated but before the colour begins to fade in the midday sun. Having said all that, if you can only find time to pick flowers at night then that is better than abandoning the idea of pressing flowers at all!

Making a flower press
You will need two pieces of plywood approximately 8 in (20 cm) square. Tape or clamp them together and drill a hole in each of the four corners, about ½ in (12 mm) in from each edge, using a drill bit that is slightly larger than the diameter of the four bolts you intend to use. These bolts should be about 3 in (7.5 cm) long so that you can fit several layers of blotting paper, newspaper and flowers into the press. You will also need four wing nuts to tighten the press once it is full.

Pressing the flowers
To fill the press you will need eleven pads of newspaper – I usually cut them as thick as the original newspaper unless it is a Sunday paper and thicker than the rest of the week's papers put together! Between these pads of newspaper you will need twenty sheets of blotting paper. Both the blotting paper and the newspaper must be cut to the size of the press or a little smaller. Cut across each of the corners so that the papers do not interfere with the bolts.

Pressing flowers is another very simple process that produces pretty additions to packaged and displayed pot pourri.

Remove any small stalks or protruding pieces from the flowers you have picked and lay them flat on the bottom layer of blotting paper. Do not let any two flowers touch each other and do not let them overlap the edge of the paper. When that layer is full, cover it with a second sheet of blotting paper followed by another pad of newspaper, and begin again with another layer of blotting paper. I usually fill a press this size with ten layers as I find that is enough to be economical but it doesn't overfill the press and endanger the end results.

Place the press in a warm part of the house with an even temperature (any more room in that airing cupboard?) Under the bed in the spare bedroom is usually a fairly safe place. Leave the press undisturbed for six weeks and then your flowers should be ready to use.

It does pay to label the press clearly with the day the flowers were pressed and maybe the contents, as I have often found a stray press in an unusual place and wondered what it contained and how long it had been there.

STORING AIR-DRIED AND PRESSED FLOWERS

When you have collected quite a few air-dried flowers or foliage, you will reach the stage where you need space to hang up more plant material. You must therefore store the dried pieces carefully so they remain undamaged until you need them. The safest way to store them is to use a long florist's box. Florists are usually quite willing to part with one as they probably have many delivered, if not every day, then certainly every week.

Tape over the holes at either end of the box, because the dried material inside acts like a magnet for small creepy crawlies and even slightly larger ones. I once found a box in my attic which contained a small family of mice, all fast asleep and curled up in a nest of dried herbs! Seriously, though, you don't want any insects to munch their way through your crop. Now lay the bunches of dried flowers or herbs in the box, with the heads all facing one way and the layers overlapping each other to cause the least possible damage.

Pressed flowers can be removed from the press after six weeks have elapsed and be stored flat in blotting paper folders. Alternatively you can keep the flowers in clear-fronted paper bags, but never use polythene bags as the flowers will sweat and go mouldy. Keep all dried flowers in a warm atmosphere with a fairly even temperature.

PRESERVING WITH SILICA GEL CRYSTALS

When you have made up your mixture and it has matured, then comes the most interesting part – decorating and displaying your pot pourri. You will find many ideas in the pages to come for easy and also more unusual ways to display your pot pourri to its best advantage. The one thing that most of the examples have in common is that the flowers decorating the surface of the mixture are all dried in silica gel crystals.

This method of drying flowers may take a little more time, money and patience than pressing or air-drying, but it really is worth while for decorating the top of the pot pourri. There is no point in using silica gel crystals to dry all the constituent parts of your pot pourri recipe as the majority of the items will be thoroughly squashed and broken during the manufacturing process.

These crystals are easily purchased from a floral specialist (see the back of the book for further details) or perhaps from a florist's shop or garden centre. If you really can't get hold of the correct crystals then as a very poor second you can use sand, borax or washing powder. I would not recommend any of these substitutes as they all take more time and give an inferior result. However, there are times when second best is all that is available, so you may have to make do with them.

An old-fashioned method

Sand has been used to dry flowers for hundreds of years. Sir Hugh Platt wrote in his book, *Delights for Ladies*, published in 1594, as follows (remember he calls rose petals, rose leaves):

'If you would performe the same wel in rose leaves, you must in rose time make a choice of such roses as are neither in the bud, nor full blowne (for these have the smoothest leaves of all other) which you must especially cull and chuse from the rest; then take sand, wash it in some change of waters, drie it thoroughly well, either in an oven, or in the sunne; and having shallow square or long boxes of four five or six inches deepe, make first an even lay of sand in the bottom upon which lay your rose leaves, one by one (so as none of the touch other) till you have covered all the sand, then strow sand upon thos leaves till you have thinly covered them all, and then make another laie of leaves as before, and so lay upon lay etc. Set this box in some warme place in a hot sunny day (and commonly in two hot sunny dayes they will be thorow dry) then tyake them out carefully with your hand without breaking. Keepe these leaves in jarre glasses, bound about with paper neere a chimney, or stove, for feare of relenting.'

He goes on to suggest that you may do likewise with other single flowers, such as pansies.

There is very little difference between the method that I would suggest today and that of Sir Hugh Platt some 400 years ago. I find silica gel crystals are far superior but then he didn't have them to hand. The crystals are white or pale blue when they are first bought and as they absorb moisture they take

Drying flowers in silica gel crystals produces a very beautiful result and the flowers can be the finishing touch to a special bowl of pot pourri.

on a pinkish shade. To remove the moisture and turn the pink crystals back to blue, spread them across a clean dry baking sheet and warm them in a cool oven until they revert to their original colour. They can therefore be used again and again for many years, which means that your original investment lasts a very long time.

Using silica gel crystals

Choose an air-tight plastic box with a lid, about 4 in (10 cm) deep, and scatter a shallow layer of crystals over the base. Then place the whole roses, or any other flower that you wish to preserve, on to the layer of crystals. Taking a small spoon, gradually cover the flower with crystals, pouring them gently into every single crevice and round the base of the flower. This is a very crucial stage as it is the way that you pour on the crystals that will determine the final shape of the flower. The crystals support the shape as well as remove the moisture.

The box will hold several flowers, depending on their size and shape, so once you have completed a layer you can cover it completely with more crystals. Replace the lid firmly on top and leave the box in a warm place for a couple of days or so. Before you remove all the contents of the box, check carefully with a teaspoon to see whether the flowers are quite dry. I usually remove one with a teaspoon and if it seems to be completely dry then the others can follow. Do not try to remove them with your fingers as you will break them: they are quite fragile.

Flowers dried in this way can look very nearly fresh, and certainly they look a lot less 'dried' than those which are dried by the air method. However, they are probably slightly more fragile and so should be handled with care. If you wish to protect them you can spray them with some matt polyurethane varnish.

Using silica gel crystals in the microwave oven

Two days is really not very long to wait for the flowers to dry. However, if you simply cannot contain yourself that long it is possible to dry the flowers in silica gel crystals in the microwave. You should use a cardboard box as opposed to a plastic container, and either place it on a shelf in your microwave or use an upturned saucer or bowl to raise the box so the moisture can escape from its base.

Cover the flowers with silica crystals in the same way as I have described above, but do not cover the box with a lid. Place it in the microwave and set to a medium setting or to defrost if that is your only alternative to high. Assuming that there is approximately 2 lb (1 kg) of crystals in the box, I usually set the oven to cook for 5–6 minutes. This time, however, will vary dramatically according to what you are drying and the output of your oven. Experiment and take careful notes so that you have the same success next time (or will know to avoid that particular pitfall!)

When the time is up, take the box out of the microwave and let it stand for about 15 minutes. You may then remove the flowers from the crystals.

Check that they are dry; if not, then cover them up again and give them a minute or so more in the microwave followed by five to ten minutes' standing time.

As you collect your dried items, store them carefully in a shallow box. They should then be kept in a warm, dry place. If your home is prone to a little humidity, then make sure the items are sprayed with polyurethane varnish before placing them on top of pot pourri mixes.

PRESERVING IN GLYCERINE

Not many of the flowers and foliage that are useful for pot pourri have to be preserved in glycerine. However, the one or two exceptions are worth making, and if you wish to use any of the following in your mixes or to decorate your container, then glycerine is the best medium to use.

Heather (all types), *Alchemilla mollis*, *Clematis tangutica* (seedheads) and rosemary (can be dried or glycerined).

There are plenty of other plant materials that preserve well with glycerine, such as beech, oak and chestnut leaves, but these are not really relevant to pot pourri manufacture.

The glycerine method

Mix glycerine with hot water in the ratio of two parts glycerine to one part water, or one part of each (both mixtures seem to work successfully). Fill a tall slim container with about 3–4 in (7.5–10 cm) of the liquid and place the stems of the item you wish to preserve into the glycerine. Make sure you have removed any surplus leaves and so on before preserving as they will take up the glycerine and then have to be discarded.

Stand the container out of strong light for several days. You will be able to see the glycerine being taken up by the plant as it subtly (or in some cases not so subtly) changes colour. Once the glycerine has travelled to the top of the stem, remove it from the jar. Keep the glycerine for reuse, and store the preserved material in a dry box. Do not store with air-dried material, however, as it may have a detrimental effect. The small drops of glycerine that sometimes appear on the stem or leaves of preserved plant material can be wiped off with a damp cloth.

The vast majority of the other items used in pot pourri such as cones, nuts and mosses, can be left to dry naturally. If there is some urgent reason why they must be instantly dried they can go into the microwave or a conventional oven, but on a very low setting. Having collected all the items that you need, the excitement can begin and you can start experimenting!

CHAPTER FOUR

Recipes and Methods for Dry Pot Pourri

In Chapter One I described the methods for making moist pot pourri, which has a strong and long-lasting scent but is not very pleasing to look at. In this chapter, on the other hand, there are many recipes for dry pot pourri, which smells just as good with the help of various essential oils and fixatives, and is a lot easier and much more fun to make. The finished result looks most attractive, with or without further decoration.

The recipes given here are meant to be guidelines for you to work from. Don't worry if, for some reason, you do not have exactly the right ingredients, because you can convert the recipe into one of your own by substituting other ingredients for the ones that are missing.

There can be myriad inspirations to set you along the path of a new recipe (please don't just use mine – try plenty of your own). A new ingredient or special occasion can set your mind ticking over, and ideas will start coming thick and fast!

Beautiful aromatic mixtures can add a special interest to any room in the house and, by making your own blends, you can choose both the colour and the fragrance.

Making your own pot pourri can be a very exciting and satisfying craft. The easiest method is probably to mix a dry pot pourri. In this type of recipe, all the ingredients are dried before being mixed together, and the fragrance is mainly provided by adding drops of essential oils, which are then given some permanence by adding a fixative, such as orris root.

The sky is the limit as far as the ingredients for this type of pot pourri are concerned. If you want to include dried carrot peel, potato peel and turnips, and call it a vegetarian pot pourri mix, then that's up to you! You can add beads and feathers, make it simple or extravagant, or do whatever takes your mood or your fancy. I will be using rather more conventional ingredients in most of the recipes given here. Please do not take any of them as gospel; there is a basic ratio of bulk to the oils and fixative, but other than that please experiment and produce creations that are all your own!

BASIC RATIO OF BULK TO OIL

As a rough guideline, for every cup of unscented botanical material, you need to add approximately 40–50 drops (or 1 scant teaspoon) of essential oil mixed with one tablespoon (15 g) of cut orris root or calamus root. This is probably a maximum amount so there is no need to exceed it unless you need a particularly long-lasting scent. Once the quantity is increased to, say, fifteen cups of botanical material in the recipe, you will need about twelve teaspoons of oil (720 drops) mixed with one cup of cut orris root.

As a reference point, these are the approximate measuring units that I have worked with in these recipes:

One teaspoon = 60 drops
One tablespoon = three teaspoons
One cup = sixteen tablespoons (8 fl oz or 225 ml)

EQUIPMENT NEEDED TO MAKE POT POURRI

Ceramic mixing bowls
Metal or glass measuring cups
Metal spoons
Pipettes (eyedroppers)
Notebook and pen
Collection of old jam jars with lids
Large storage jars

The basic equipment that you will need is not very expensive and is often already in the kitchen cupboards. Always use glass or ceramic mixing bowls and stainless steel or glass measuring equipment (I use an old heat-proof glass measuring jug). Never use wood or plastic as they can both retain smells long after the pot pourri is finished! A collection of old jam or coffee jars with clean lids will be useful for storing the blends of oil and orris or calamus root, but more of that later.

You will need some large jars in which to keep the finished pot pourri mix while it is maturing. Old-fashioned sweet jars or large storage jars are excellent for this, and if you can find dark-coloured glass versions, then so much the better, as they keep out the light and prevent the colours fading. Having said that, it is not easy to find such gems, so buy the best substitutes that you can, and make sure they have well-fitting lids. If the jars are made from clear glass, then you must age the pot pourri out of direct light in a cupboard or other convenient dark place.

Large old metal spoons are useful for stirring the mixture, and you will need a notebook and pen for jotting down your versions of the recipes and general notes. Finally, some pipettes (eyedroppers) are invaluable when dispensing the essential oils. Make sure you buy several as it is far easier to have one for each oil, carefully labelled, than to keep cleaning your one pipette each time you use it. Some small bottles of oil have a drop dispenser incorporated into the neck of the bottle, but I would still recommend buying some pipettes as well.

Before we start the interesting part of this chapter, with its recipes and ideas, I must sound a quick word of warning. The oils used in pot pourri are very strong and should be kept well away from children. You should also store the general ingredients away from very young children; I doubt that they would eat very many of them, but they could make a wonderfully interesting mess all over the house if they felt so inclined! Allergies do sometimes occur with these natural ingredients, so it might be worth wearing a mask and working with good ventilation, such as several open windows.

BASIC METHOD FOR MAKING DRY POT POURRI

Mixing together the essential oil and fixative

Using one of your collection of clean jam jars, pour in and mix together ½ cup or 8 tablespoons of cut orris root with 6 teaspoons or ¼ fluid ounce (350 drops approximately) of essential oil. Write that particular fragrance on a label and stick it on the jar immediately.

It is important to use cut orris root, and not the powdered variety, as the small pieces of orris root distribute themselves efficiently. The powder just gives everything a dusty appearance.

Make up a reasonable selection of jars of oil and fixative and label each one clearly with the individual fragrance. Do not mix different fragrances within one jar – the mixing will take place later on! These jars can be made up well in advance of the rest of your pot pourri mixing as they need a few days to mature. Leave the jars in a dark place.

Collecting the ingredients

Once your fixative mixture has matured, collect together the ingredients needed for the recipe you are following. If you don't have a particular ingredient then substitute the same weight or volume of another ingredient.

As the oils will be providing most of the scent, it is not crucial to have exactly the same component parts as stated in a recipe. However, if you are lacking a particularly fragrant ingredient, such as lemon peel or a herb, then you may want to add a little lemon oil, or whichever one is appropriate, and fixative to balance the smell. Let your nose decide!

Mixing together the ingredients
Once you have assembled all your ingredients, you can mix them with the oil and fixative mixture in a large ceramic or glass mixing bowl. Do not use your hands or a wooden spoon, but ensure you use a metal spoon.

Maturing the mixture
Once all the ingredients are combined, fill one of your large storage jars and again label it immediately with the name of the pot pourri. Leave it in a warm place, out of direct light, for between two to four weeks. The mixture should be stirred twice a week (this is important): either give the jar a good shake (which tends to damage the larger ingredients) or just tip the mixture out into a bowl and back into the jar again.

After two or three weeks have a good sniff: if the smell seems strong enough, and you are happy with the blend of scents, then you are ready to display your creation! See Chapter Five onwards for some display ideas.

RECIPES WITH A ROSE BASE

For many centuries, the rose has been a very popular flower with perfume and pot pourri makers. The majority of the early recipes all use roses as their base and I see no reason to alter this. Rose petals, whole roses and rose-buds all look wonderful in a pot pourri mix and give a fabulous start to the perfume blend.

Rose garden pot pourri
The contents of this recipe were inspired by a visit to a wonderful formal rose garden, with its neatly clipped box hedges and lavender planted under the standard roses.

4 cups rose-buds (in shades of pink, cream and red)
4 cups rose petals (colours as above)
2 cups lavender flowers

1 cup golden privet leaves
1 cup box leaves (Buxus sempervirens)
8 tablespoons rose oiled fixative
4 tablespoons lavender oiled fixative

Combine all the ingredients well and allow to mature. Decorate with whole rose heads dried in silica crystals and tiny bundles of lavender tied with narrow pink ribbon.

These gorgeous tiny rosebuds make this particular mixture very special and would look very pretty on a dressing table or bedside table.

Rosie lee

Herbal teas smell as delicious as they taste, and when I decided to experiment with them this name came to mind. 'Rosie lee' is cockney rhyming slang for tea!

6 cups rose petals (in shades of pink, red or peach)
2 cups camomile flowers
2 cups rose hips
2 cups rose leaves
1 cup rose hip herbal tea (dry)
½ cup orange peel cut into thin strips
8 tablespoons rose oiled fixative
2 tablespoons sweet orange oiled fixative
2 tablespoons tea rose oiled fixative

Combine all the ingredients and allow to mature. To decorate, use some glycerined bunches of rose hips, small rose-buds and twists of dried orange peel.

Rose Marie

I've always been touched by the sentiments in Country and Western songs, so this mixture seemed ideal!

8 cups yellow rose petals (dried in silica crystals)
3 cups rosemary leaves
1 cup cracked nutmegs
1 cup oak moss
1 cup small rose leaves
10 tablespoons rose oiled fixative
2 tablespoons rosemary oiled fixative
1 tablespoon patchouli oiled fixative

Combine all the ingredients and allow to mature. Decorate with whole nutmegs, yellow rose-buds and rose heads dried in silica crystals, and little bunches of rosemary tied with thin yellow ribbons.

Secret love

We all associate red roses with love, valentines and romance, and in the secret language of flowers the red rose, not surprisingly, represents true love.

8 cups bright red rose petals
2 cups alpine strawberry leaves
2 cups oak moss
2 cups silver artemisia leaves
7 tablespoons rose oiled fixative
2 tablespoons musk oiled fixative
2 tablespoons patchouli oiled fixative
2 tablespoons ambergris oiled fixative

Combine all the ingredients and allow to mature. To decorate, add some whole red roses and some alpine strawberries and their leaves, all dried in silica crystals.

Wild rose

The wild roses that grow in the hedgerows of England during June are quite beautiful and are worth preserving in silica crystals even if you only collect one or two. They don't have the same heavy scent as the old-fashioned roses but they do have a special simplicity of their own. This recipe is inspired by English hedgerows!

4 cups cream rose petals (preferably dried in silica crystals)
4 cups blackberry leaves
2 cups honeysuckle flowers
½ cup elderberries
½ cup hawthorn berries
1 cup rose hips
8 tablespoons rose oiled fixative
2 tablespoons apple oiled fixative
2 tablespoons honeysuckle oiled fixative

Combine all the ingredients and allow to mature. Decorate with wild roses and honeysuckle flowers dried in silica crystals.

Cottage flora

England's cottage gardens played an important role in the history of gardening, and many of the flowers that were so popular then are being grown again in greater numbers today. All the ingredients in this pot pourri can come from your garden, and the gentle colours are a happy reminder of summer.

4 cups pale blue delphiniums
4 cups pink roses
2 cups peony petals
2 cups 'Doris' pinks
2 cups lavender
4 tablespoons lavender oiled fixative
8 tablespoons rose oiled fixative
2 tablespoons carnation oiled fixative

Combine all the ingredients and allow to mature. To decorate, add pale blue delphiniums, whole 'Doris' pinks and a couple of whole pink rose heads, all dried in silica crystals.

Pot pourri mixtures can easily be colour coordinated with either the room they are intended for or as decor for a special occasion.

The enormous range of ingredients and oils is virtually unlimited so the creative and artistic choices are yours!

RECIPES WITH A HERB BASE

Herbs have been used for their healing and fragrant properties for many years, and make a lovely base for pot pourri that has a fresh outdoor smell. Herbs combine well with fruity smells, spicy smells and some flower fragrances. Try drying a selection of herbs from your garden and see how your personal blend develops.

Tussie mussie

A tussie mussie is a posy of flowers and herbs, made originally to ward off the evil smells caused by plague and lack of sewers. These posies gradually became bearers of secret messages using the language of flowers and today can be given as a gift of friendship.

3 cups rose petals
3 cups scented geranium leaves
2 cups lavender flowers
1/2 cup mint leaves
1/2 cup rosemary leaves
4 tablespoons rose oiled fixative
2 tablespoons rose geranium oiled fixative
2 tablespoons lavender oiled fixative
1/2 tablespoon clove oiled fixative
1/2 tablespoon nutmeg oiled fixative

Combine all the ingredients and allow to mature. Decorate with three silica dried geranium leaves in the centre of the dish with a whole rose (also dried in silica crystals) in the middle to look like a miniature posy.

White magic

Herbs have long been connected with good magic (as well as bad).

3 cups white hydrangea petals
2 cups white cherry blossom
1 cup rosemary leaves
1 cup lemon thyme leaves
1 cup myrtle leaves and flowers
1 cup feverfew flowers
2 cups oak moss
1/2 cup lemon grass rings
1/2 cup star anise (whole stars)
5 tablespoons lily of the valley oiled fixative
3 tablespoons violet oiled fixative
2 tablespoons thyme oiled fixative
2 tablespoons rosemary oiled fixative

Combine all the ingredients and allow to mature. To decorate, add some violets or sprays of lily of the valley dried in silica crystals. Try arranging some anise stars on the top and a small group of lemon grass rings.

Monastery garden

Monks were the most educated members of any community at one time, and they tended the herb gardens and passed down their herbal remedies to the next generation.

3 cups chive flowers
2 cups silver artemisia leaves
2 cups bergamot flowers and leaves
2 cups marjoram flowers
2 cups lavender flowers
½ cup juniper berries
½ cup sandalwood chips
4 tablespoons lavender oiled fixative
3 tablespoons thyme oiled fixative
1½ tablespoons frankincense oiled fixative
1½ tablespoons myrrh oiled fixative
2 tablespoons lemon verbena oiled fixative

Combine all the ingredients and allow to mature. Decorate with tiny bundles of herbs and chive flowers dried in silica crystals.

Parsley, sage, rosemary and thyme

'Scarborough Fair' in one of my favourite songs, and I thought the herbs mentioned in it would make a good kitchen pot pourri!

2 cups parsley
2 cups purple sage leaves
2 cups rosemary leaves
2 cups lemon thyme
2 cups pale pink globe amaranth
1½ tablespoons sage oiled fixative
2½ tablespoons lemon oiled fixative
1½ tablespoons rosemary oiled fixative
1½ tablespoons basil oiled fixative
1½ tablespoons thyme oiled fixative
1½ tablespoons mint oiled fixative.

Mix all the ingredients and allow to mature. To decorate, display in a basket lined with a gingham cloth and place a couple of glycerined sprigs of rosemary on top, tied together with a co-ordinating ribbon.

RECIPES WITH A FRUITY AND SPICY BASE

Fruit-based pot pourri mixtures are very popular today. The best selling fragrances in our experience have been peach and strawberry, whatever the form they take. So, if you are unsure of someone's taste in perfume and you want to choose a gift that will be well received, then a fruit-based recipe is bound to be a winner!

Spiced autumn pears

We have an enormous old pear tree in our garden that produces a type of pear called honey pears, or so I am reliably informed by my grandmother. In the late summer when the tree is groaning under the weight of juicy pears, the garden is filled with brightly coloured butterflies who seem to love the pears as much as we do.

1 cup elderflowers	2 cups small pieces peeled ginger root
4 cups yellow rose petals	1 cup cracked nutmegs
2 cups oak moss	8 tablespoons pear oiled fixative
1 cup crushed cinnamon sticks	2 tablespoons ginger oiled fixative
1 cup allspice berries	2 tablespoons cinnamon oiled fixative

Combine all the ingredients and allow to mature. To decorate, dry some slices of pear and arrange with large pieces of peeled root ginger on top of the pot pourri.

Apple harvest

4 cups dried apple slices cut in half	1/2 cup cloves
2 cups oak moss	1 cup applemint leaves
2 cups cut mistletoe herb	8 tablespoons apple oiled fixative
2 cups red globe amaranth flowers	2 tablespoons cinnamon oiled fixative
1/2 cup crushed cinnamon sticks	2 tablespoons clove oiled fixative

Combine all the ingredients and allow to mature. To decorate, lay some of the best whole apple slices and sticks of cinnamon on the top.

Strawberry tea

Whenever I smell strawberries I always think of a traditional family tea-time in the garden during the summer. Scones and cakes, strawberries and cream and children with grubby knees!

4 cups pink and red rose-buds	8 tablespoons strawberry oiled fixative
2 cups pink and red rose petals	2 tablespoons sweet orange oiled fixative
4 cups strawberry leaves	1 scant tablespoon black pepper oiled fixative
1 cup black peppercorns	

Combine all the ingredients and allow to mature. To decorate, add some strawberry flowers and leaves, or berries, dried in silica crystals, and a few pressed lawn daisies.

Peach crumble

Peach is always a popular scent and so is cinnamon, so when they are combined they make a delicious perfume.

4 cups apricot globe amaranth
2 cups camomile flowers
2 cups marigold flowers
2 cups peachy rose petals
2 cups broken cinnamon sticks

1 cup halved vanilla pods
9 tablespoons peach oiled fixative
2 tablespoons vanilla oiled fixative
2 tablespoons cinnamon oiled fixative

Combine all the ingredients and allow to mature. When matured, decorate with a couple of whole peach rose heads and a small bundle of cinnamon sticks and vanilla pods tied with a peach ribbon.

Summer lemonade

There are many lemon-scented herbs and plants in the garden during the summer, and the scent of lemons is always invigorating and refreshing. This pot pourri has a sweet minty overtone that prevents it smelling too much like a fresh and invigorating household cleanser!

2 cups lemon verbena leaves
1 cup lemon thyme
1 cup lemon balm
2 cups lemon mint (Citrata) *leaves*

2 cups thin strips of lemon peel
2 cups lemon scented geranium leaves
8 tablespoons lemon oiled fixative
2 tablespoons mint oiled fixative

Combine all the ingredients and allow to mature. To decorate, add rings of dried lemon peel. Make these by slicing across a lemon and removing all the flesh from the middle, leaving an empty circle of peel. Dry these as for apple slices (slowly in a low oven). Overlap three rings in the centre of the dish of pot pourri.

Orange blossom

Orange blossom is a very romantic flower; it always makes me think of weddings, sunny days and beautiful dresses. The perfume mix here is lovely for a bedroom or bathroom.

3 cups 'Paper White' narcissus flowers
2 cups honeysuckle flowers
2 cups orange blossoms
2 cups Kerria *flowers*
2 cups bergamot leaves

1 cup small variegated ivy leaves
8 tablespoons sweet orange oiled fixative
3 tablespoons neroli oiled fixative
1 tablespoon bergamot oiled fixative

Combine all the ingredients and allow to mature. To decorate, dry some kumquats and small privet or pittosporum leaves and arrange on the top of the pot pourri.

COLOUR CO-ORDINATED POT POURRI

Many people want a pot pourri to blend with their room decor. It is very straightforward to make a completely pink or blue mix, but make sure you add a slight contrast, otherwise it can look rather boring. Green leaves often show off the colours well, but you could introduce some cream or white, grey or even a completely contrasting colour depending on the colour scheme involved. Here are some examples.

Greengage summer
The colour scheme here is green with some white daisies for contrast – very summery!

3 cups hop flowers
2 cups chunks of lime peel
1 cup cardamom pods
2 cups large lawn daisies (silica dried)
2 cups eucalyptus leaves
1 cup rue leaves
8 tablespoons plum oiled fixative
2 tablespoons cinnamon oiled fixative
1 tablespoon clove oiled fixative
1 tablespoon lime oiled fixative

Combine all the ingredients and allow to mature. To decorate, take several large silica dried daisies or other white flowers, such as *Achillea ptarmica* 'The Pearl', and arrange in a ring like a daisy chain around the edge and in the middle of the pot pourri.

Pink champagne
This is a celebration pot pourri for special occasions such as weddings or anniversaries. It takes a little more time to dry all the ingredients with silica crystals but in this case it is worth it.

4 cups silica dried pink rose-buds
2 cups silica dried violet leaves
2 cups silica dried peony petals
2 cups silica dried pink fuchsias
2 cups silica dried pink hydrangeas
8 tablespoons rose oiled fixative
2 tablespoons violet oiled fixative
2 tablespoons carnation oiled fixative

Combine all the ingredients very gently because silica dried items are not as robust as the ones that have been air-dried. To decorate, take a whole peony that has been silica dried and place it to one side of the pot pourri, with a few violet leaves to set it off.

Lady of the lake

This collection of blues and mauves is very pretty and gives a subtle aroma to any room in the house.

2 cups mixed blue delphiniums
*2 cups love-in-a-mist (*Nigella*)*
2 cups lavender
2 cups 'Blue Moon' rose petals
2 cups dark blue mallow petals
2 cups oak moss
4 tablespoons jasmine oiled fixative
4 tablespoons lavender oiled fixative
2 tablespoons ylang-ylang oiled fixative

Combine all the ingredients and allow to mature. To decorate, take some silica dried borage flowers, or any other small blue flowers, and arrange in a broad band diagonally across the middle of the dish.

Red hot embers

This is a really striking red mixture that would be a good Christmas mix or would brighten up any dull corner.

2 cups poppy petals
2 cups bright red rose petals
2 cups red potentillas ('Miss Willmott' or 'Gibson's Scarlet')
2 cups berberis or cotinus leaves
1 cup red sandalwood
1 cup dried chillies
1 cup hawthorn berries or rose hips
4 tablespoons rosewood oiled fixative
2 tablespoons vanilla oiled fixative
2 tablespoons bergamot oiled fixative
1 tablespoon ginger oiled fixative
1 tablespoon sweet orange oiled fixative

Combine all the ingredients and allow to mature. To decorate, add some bright red de Caen anemones with some green leaves or large purple cotinus leaves.

SEASONAL POT POURRI MIXES

One of the bonuses of home-made pot pourri is that you can change your mixture and store or recycle it as you wish. The cost is far less than buying commercially made mixes, so you can be more extravagant and change your mixtures with the seasons.

Spring recipes

I always think of spring when anyone mentions *The Wind in the Willows* by

Kenneth Grahame, because of the quote 'Oh, hang spring cleaning', from Ratty. I couldn't agree with him more!

Wind in the willows
4 cups 'Paper White' narcissus flowers
2 cups violet flowers
2 cups violet leaves
2 cups silica dried primroses
2 cups mimosa blooms
1 cup thin strips grapefruit peel
8 tablespoons neroli oiled fixative
1 tablespoon ambergris oiled fixative
1 tablespoon bergamot oiled fixative
2 tablespoons violet oiled fixative

Combine all the ingredients and allow to mature. To decorate, silica dry some sprays of mimosa, violet leaves and primroses to place around the edge of the bowl.

Queen of the May
Maypole dancing and choosing a girl to be the May queen or 'Queen of the May' is a popular custom in many countries. Here is a pot pourri to celebrate Maytime.

4 cups pink cherry blossom
4 cups periwinkle flowers
2 cups dark pink rose petals
1 cup blue mallow flowers
1 cup small raspberry leaves
½ cup sliced vanilla pods
4 tablespoons rose geranium oiled fixative
4 tablespoons jasmine oiled fixative
2 tablespoons lavender oiled fixative
1 tablespoon vanilla oiled fixative
1 tablespoon ambergris oiled fixative

Combine all the ingredients and allow to mature. To decorate, place some silica dried cherry blossom and periwinkle flowers on the surface of the pot pourri with some bows or curls of pink and pale blue ribbon.

Summer pot pourri recipes
Summer is the easiest time to create a pot pourri recipe because there are so many varieties of flowers and plants blooming away in the garden then. These are two of my favourites. The first, Secret Garden, was named after the book, which is one of our family's favourites. The second is named after

This summery pot pourri mix has been displayed in a large shell, which underlines the seashore theme of the contents.

64

one of my favourite summer pastimes, wondering along local beaches with our spaniel, collecting treasures. I don't know who collects more treasures, we humans or the dog!

Secret garden pot pourri

4 cups mock orange flowers
2 cups pink larkspur flowers
2 cups single pink roses
2 cups 'Doris' pinks or similar
1 cup oak moss
1 cup strawberry leaves

4 tablespoons neroli oiled fixative
2 tablespoons ylang-ylang oiled fixative
2 tablespoons patchouli oiled fixative
2 tablespoons bergamot oiled fixative
2 tablespoons rose geranium oiled fixative

Combine all the ingredients and allow to mature. To decorate, take some whole mock orange flowers and pink rose heads that have been silica dried and arrange them in a posy in the middle of the pot pourri.

Beachcomber's paradise

6 cups mixed blue and white larkspur
  flowers
1 cup cedar chips
1 cup quassia chips
1 cup 1 in (2.5 cm) lengths of liquorice
  root
2 cups pearly shells

4 tablespoons lavender oiled fixative
1 tablespoon juniper oiled fixative
1 tablespoon rosewood oiled fixative
1 tablespoon pine oiled fixative
2 tablespoons vanilla oiled fixative

Combine all the ingredients and allow to mature. To decorate, place a band of wood chips, either cedar or quassia, along one edge of the container and scatter shells along the length of the wood.

Autumn or fall recipes

There are so many crops being harvested in the autumn, such as fruits, flowers, cones and nuts, that a fruity-based pot pourri seems inevitable! Harvest Moon has a fruit base whilst Amber Glow concentrates on the warm colours of the leaves at this time of year.

Harvest moon

2 cups apple slices cut in half
1 cup costus flowers
2 cups hibiscus flowers
2 cups strips of orange peel
2 cups oak moss
1 cup lemon grass rings
1 cup acorns

1 cup peach-coloured rose petals
4 tablespoons apple oiled fixative
2 tablespoons peach oiled fixative
1 tablespoon pear oiled fixative
1 tablespoon sweet orange oiled fixative
1 tablespoon ginger oiled fixative
2 tablespoons cinnamon oiled fixative

Combine all the ingredients and allow to mature. To decorate, use dried apple slices brushed with cinnamon oil, cinnamon sticks and kumquats stuck with cloves like tiny pomanders.

Amber glow

2 cups dahlia or zinnia petals in bronze
    colourings
2 cups marigold petals
2 cups small autumnal leaves
2 cups tangerine potentillas
1 cup gold Achillea flowers
½ cup mace
½ cup chillies
½ cup vanilla pods

½ cup cracked nutmegs
1 cup peeled ginger root
4 tablespoons patchouli oiled fixative
3 tablespoons neroli oiled fixative
1 tablespoon ginger oiled fixative
2 tablespoons sweet orange oiled
    fixative
2 tablespoons bitter almond oiled
    fixative

Combine all the ingredients and allow to mature. Decorate with whole silica dried dahlias and autumn leaves.

Winter pot pourri

Although there are many other festive pot pourri recipes later on in the book, I couldn't resist putting this really special recipe first as it's one of my favourites!

We three kings

3 cups dark red petals or rose-buds
2 cups Nigella seed heads gilded or
    sprayed gold
1 cup purple globe amaranth flowers
2 cups costus flowers
1 cup whole star anise
1 cup broken cinnamon sticks

4 tablespoons rose oiled fixative
1 tablespoon musk oiled fixative
2 tablespoons cinnamon oiled fixative
1 tablespoon pine oiled fixative
1 tablespoon frankincense oiled fixative
1 tablespoon myrrh oiled fixative

Combine all the ingredients and allow to mature. Since it's Christmas, you can really go to town with a large bowl of this pot pourri edged with small pine cones, bundles of cinnamon sticks tied with gold cord and groups of the gilded Nigella seed heads.

CHAPTER FIVE

Displaying your Pot Pourri

This chapter contains many ideas for unusual pot pourri mixes and also more examples of ways to display your creations, to make the most of their colours, contents and fragrance.

In many cases you need only reserve some of the ingredients – usually the prime specimens – and scatter them across the top of the pot pourri. But it is also fun to think of a theme for your display, such as the sea shore or perhaps something that blends with your decor, and to design your pot pourri display around that.

Christmas and winter, log fires and pine cones are always very inspirational and you will find several Christmassy ideas here, which I hope will lead you on to more ideas of your own. These ideas are fine for those of us for whom Christmas comes during the winter season but in Australia it's high summer and so there are some summery native Australian ideas here to compensate!

I hope that once I have given you the germ of a few ideas, your creative ability will go into overdrive, inspiring you to think up dozens of new ideas for displaying your own pot pourri mixes as well as mine.

The choice of suitable containers is huge; almost anything can be used, depending upon where you wish to display your mixture.

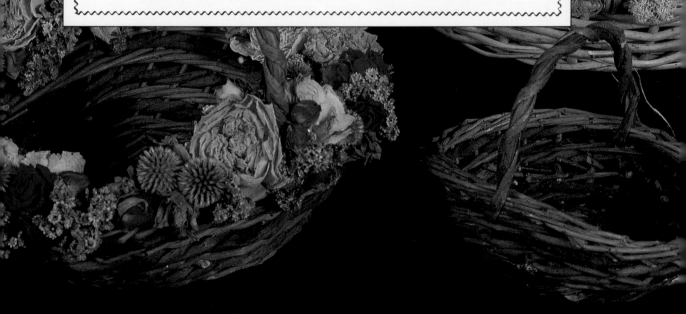

FLOWER-EDGED BASKETS

One of the easiest ways to make a container for your pot pourri is to take a pretty basket and attach silica or air-dried flowers around the edges or at the base of the handle. You could repeat the ingredients that you have used in the pot pourri, except perhaps you might have air-dried the material for the actual recipe and used silica crystals to dry the more fragile of the flowers for the decoration.

Alternatively, if you don't want to repeat the pot pourri ingredients, you could pick a colour theme from the mix and use, for example, more blue flowers to accompany a blue and mauve mixture. Sometimes the pot pourri has been made for a special occasion, such as a wedding or anniversary (of which more later), in which case you might place larger, more beautiful flowers around the edge of the basket with smaller air-dried flowers contained in the bulk of the pot pourri.

Peaches and dream

This pot pourri and its container were designed for a pretty bedroom, perhaps to sit on a chest of drawers or a feminine dressing table. Many people have this peach and cream colour combination somewhere in their homes, and it makes a good decorative accent in the same way as a dried flower arrangement would, but has the added bonus of a dreamy fragrance.

2 cups peach rose petals
2 cups cream rose petals
1 cup cream globe amaranth flowers
1 cup dried peach slices (or substitute small apple slices)
½ cup chopped vanilla pods
½ cup cracked nutmegs
1 cup small cinnamon sticks (cut in half if necessary)
4 tablespoons peach oiled fixative
2 tablespoons vanilla oiled fixative
2 tablespoons neroli or orange blossom oiled fixative

Combine all the ingredients and allow to mature. From choice, the rose petals should all be dried in silica crystals as this makes them far smoother and means that the whole mix looks prettier.

Choose a medium-sized basket with a mid-brown or golden colouring. (If it's a bleached willow basket then dye it with wood dye.) Then, using a hot-glue gun (available from most DIY stores), fix your choice of flowers around the edge of the basket. In the example shown in the photograph, I have used peachy 'Gerda' roses mixed with some 'Champagne' roses, and in between these I have glued loops of old lace and pearls. The pearls come in a continuous string, and are usually sold in craft stores or shops with a good range of ribbons. As a final touch I have glued some gypsophila all round the basket to add to the airy feminine feel.

The same display could be made with a pink colour theme and called Strawberries and Dream!

AUSTRALIAN NATIVE FLOWERS

Many lovely flowers that are native to Australia dry beautifully to make a very dramatic pot pourri and display. As well as having some very special friends in Australia I also have a very soft spot for koala bears, so I've named this pot pourri after them!

Koala keepsake
4 cups eucalyptus leaves
2 cups dried kangaroo paws
2 cups mimosa
2 cups Craspedia globosa *flowers*
1 cup eucalyptus fruit
1 cup small orange Helichrysum *heads*
2 cups oak moss
2 tablespoons musk oiled fixative
2 tablespoons sweet orange oiled fixative
1 tablespoon juniper oiled fixative
2 tablespoons eucalyptus oiled fixative
1 tablespoon ginger oiled fixative
1 tablespoon vanilla oiled fixative
1 tablespoon cedar oiled fixative

Combine all the ingredients and allow to mature. To decorate, take a large dark basket and, using a hot-glue gun, attach sprays of silica dried mimosa, eucalyptus leaves, *Dryandra* heads, *Craspedia globosa* heads and small orange/salmon *Helichrysum* heads. If you are as daft as I am then include a couple of tiny koala bears!

Although those are the more obvious flowers of Australia, there are also many others that would fit into any colour scheme that you wanted. The recipe below uses *Helipterum*, which is widely available in most countries as a dried flower.

Rosy sunray
3 cups pink Helipterum roseum *flowers*
3 cups violet leaves
2 cups violet flowers
2 cups pink heather heads
2 cups large white daisies
4 tablespoons rose oiled fixative
2 tablespoons patchouli oiled fixative
4 tablespoons violet oiled fixative
1 tablespoon strawberry oiled fixative

Combine all the ingredients and allow to mature. To decorate, fill a large wooden bowl with the pot pourri and scatter large silica dried daisies on top.

Baskets can be edged with dried flowers and other ingredients to make beautiful containers that blend with the pot pourri.

Here a wedding bouquet has been dried and the flowers used to edge this basket, which contains other flowers dried from the church arrangements and made into pot pourri.

WEDDINGS AND SPECIAL ANNIVERSARIES

No matter where you are in the world, weddings and anniversaries are a very important part of life. Flowers are intrinsically tied to the wedding ceremony, and drying the flowers used in bouquets and decorations is a lovely way to preserve the happy memories. Turning the wedding flowers into pot pourri is a more unusual way to preserve them, and this pot pourri can then be added to as life progresses, using flowers given to celebrate the arrival of a new baby, and so on.

There will usually be more than just the bride's bouquet in the way of flowers at a wedding, so some flowers from the reception, the bride's parents' garden or even the church make an excellent basis for the pot pourri. From choice, I would rather keep the bride's bouquet to dry in silica crystals and use these special flowers to decorate the top of the pot pourri.

There are many, many flowers that can be included in the pot pourri mix, as their scent is not important. The main scent can be chosen by the bride and added in the form of essential oils. Colour schemes are often important and can reflect the colour scheme of the wedding, and small baskets or containers can also be made up to give as gifts to the bridesmaids, or the mothers of the bride and groom.

Bridal blush

Here, the colour scheme is one of the palest pinks, champagne and creamy ivory, and the scents chosen by this particular bride were gardenia, lily of the valley and carnation.

4 cups pale pink or cream peony petals
4 cups palest pink and champagne coloured rose-buds
2 cups pink and white heather
1 cup mixed pearls and crystals
2 cups small variegated ivy leaves
6 tablespoons gardenia oiled fixative
2 tablespoons lily of the valley oiled fixative
2 tablespoons carnation oiled fixative
2 tablespoons rose oiled fixative

Combine all the ingredients and allow to mature. The pot pourri could be displayed in many ways, but I would suggest drying the best flowers from the bride's bouquet in silica crystals. In this case they included small Singapore orchids, roses, spray carnations and ivy. The basket can be sprayed cream or white and lined with some bridal fabric. The silica dried flowers could then just be scattered across the top of the pot pourri or fixed to the sides with a hot glue gun. Other methods, such as wiring, can cause massive frustrations when you shatter the delicate blooms while trying to wire them on to the basket!

Bridal shower

This is a recipe for natural confetti – with luck, some churches won't mind if a completely bio-degradeable confetti is thrown in their grounds. As it is perfumed you could make it up into little lace favours and sachets for the reception instead of throwing it over the bride. Many brides have problems with friends adding confetti to their suitcase, but at least this would make their clothes smell sweet even if it does cause some embarrassment at the hotel!

All the ingredients have a special significance or meaning which I have put in brackets after the amount of each ingredient listed.

1 cup marjoram flowers (for health and happiness)
1 cup rosemary (for remembrance)
4 cups rose petals (for love and unity)
1 cup mint leaves (for virtue)
1 cup dill flowers (for luck)
1 cup tiny ivy leaves (for fidelity)
2 cups pansies (for loving thoughts)
6 tablespoons rose oiled fixative
2 tablespoons sweet orange oiled fixative
1 tablespoon ginger oiled fixative
1 tablespoon violet oiled fixative

Combine all the ingredients and allow to mature. The confetti can either be tied into small lace bags or you could use pretty lace-edged handkerchiefs instead. Take a handkerchief, place a couple of tablespoons or so (according to the size of the handkerchief) in the middle, pull up the corners and edges and tie with ribbon to match the colour of the bridesmaids' dresses. If these will be given as favours at the wedding, you could decorate the ribbons with a couple of tiny silica dried pansies or violas and some sprigs of herbs.

Sugar almond pot pourri

This is another recipe that would be an ideal filler for small wedding favours. It is traditional in Italy, and now in many other countries too, to place sugar almonds tied into little net *bonbonières* on the wedding tables. This recipe is based on that tradition and should be presented in the same way.

2 cups pale pink larkspur flowers
2 cups white larkspur flowers
2 cups pale blue larkspur flowers
2 cups cream globe amaranth flowers
2 cups pale pink globe amaranth flowers
4 tablespoons vanilla oiled fixative
4 tablespoons almond oiled fixative
2 tablespoons neroli oiled fixative

Combine all the ingredients and allow to mature. You will need net in whichever colour blends with the colour scheme of the wedding, such as pink and white, or pink, white and blue. Cut out circles of net 9 in (22.5 cm) in diameter and, using at least two thicknesses of net (three, perhaps, if you are using three colours), arrange them one on top of each other. Place a couple of tablespoons of pot pourri in the centre of each pile of net circles. Take up the edges of each one and tie with a narrow ribbon. The ribbons can then be decorated with pearls, crystals or some of the tiny flowers used in the pot pourri mixture. These favours can be placed individually on tables, or you could arrange a selection in a silver basket or dish so that the ribbons and decorations show to their best advantage.

POT POURRI BASKETS FOR BRIDESMAIDS

Instead of posies of fresh flowers, bridesmaids can carry little baskets filled with pot pourri and edged with dried or fresh flowers. The bonus of using dried flowers is that these baskets can be kept for ever, whereas the fresh flowers will not last very long. This particular recipe was made up for a tiny bridesmaid to carry and hence the name, as she really did look like a little princess.

The inspiration for the contents of this pot pourri came from an old spell 'To Enable One To See The Fairies'. It may only be a bit of fun today perhaps, but who knows? I will quote it anyway!

To enable one to see the fairies
A pint of sallet oyle and put it into a vial glasse, and first wash it with rose-water and marygolde water, the flowers to be gathered towards the east. Wash it till the oyle becomes white, then put it into the glasse, and then put thereto the buds of hollyhocke, the flowers of marygolde, the flowers or toppes of wilde thyme, the buds of young hazel and the thyme must be gathered near the side of a hill where the fairies used to be, and take the grasse of a fairy throne, then all these put into the oyle in the glasse and sette it to dissolve three dayes in the sun, and then keep it for thy use.

Fairy princess
4 cups rose petals
2 cups marigold petals
2 cups dried hollyhock petals
1 cup thyme leaves and flowers
1 cup small hazel leaves
2 cups oak moss
4 tablespoons rose oiled fixative
2 tablespoons marigold oiled fixative
1 tablespoon thyme oiled fixative
1 tablespoon vanilla oiled fixative
2 tablespoons violet oiled fixative

Combine all the ingredients and allow to mature. To make up a basket for the bridesmaid to carry, pick a medium-sized basket (depending on the size of the bridesmaid!) with a fairly tall handle as this makes it easier for her to hold on to it during the service.

The basket can be left natural or sprayed with a pale wash of cream. I left the basket its natural dark colour but sprayed it with a florists' pearlized spray which gave a beautiful sparkle whenever the light caught the pearly sheen. Remember the theme is fairies – this particular bridesmaid wanted wings, let alone pearlized spray! The basket was lined with an offcut of pale peach silk from the bridesmaid's dress, which prevented the pot pourri dropping through the gaps in the basket's weave.

Hollyhock flowers, whole marigolds and pale 'Champagne' roses, all dried in silica crystals, were then attached to the sides and edges of the basket. I glycerined some hazel catkins when they were still very tight and then attached them to the edge of the basket as well, to hang down the sides. Also included in the design were some wired crystals and pearls to link up with the pearly sheen on the basket.

This particular bridesmaid wore a matching head-dress and the older girls carried hoops (fairy rings?) of dried roses, marigolds and catkins. You could, however, just make the pot pourri as a bridal gift and include the old spell for fun!

POT POURRI WITH TOPIARY TREES

Topiary trees make a delightful addition to living rooms or dining rooms, or any other room where one has the space. Glass containers are not often associated with dried flowers as they are not as easy to work with as baskets or more natural containers, but some very exciting effects can be achieved using glass, as can be seen in the photograph.

Having decided that I was going to make a large topiary tree, I wanted a more unusual base than the terracotta pots that work so well but have been seen so many times. I often fill this glass tank with coloured marbles (and water!) when arranging fresh flowers in it, and this inspired the idea of a stone and root pot pourri to fill the base. The tree itself must be rooted in cement or plaster of Paris, so I placed the small branch, which served as the trunk, in an empty baked bean can and filled around it with plaster of Paris. Don't rinse out your utensils in the sink after mixing the plaster of Paris as it can block the drains. (I wonder how I know that?)

A ball of florists' foam for dried flowers, 3½ in (9 cm) in diameter, was then placed on top of the branch and the sphere filled with dried flower heads and seed heads. The baked bean can was then covered in green sphagnum moss, just in case it ever became visible, and placed in the centre of the glass tank. The pot pourri was then poured around the can and over the top to give a heaped effect.

The faraway tree

Enid Blyton fans will recognize the inspiration for this title. The ingredients are all mosses, woods and roots, as befits the base of a tree.

2 cups oak moss
1 cup small stones or gravel
1 cup cedar chips
1 cup sandalwood chips
1 cup small pieces of peeled ginger root
1 cup small pieces of liquorice root
2 cups costus flowers
1 cup hawthorn berries
1 cup lemon grass rings
2 tablespoons lavender oiled fixative
1 tablespoon cedar oiled fixative
1 tablespoon juniper oiled fixative
1 tablespoon sandalwood oiled fixative
1 tablespoon pine oiled fixative
2 tablespoons violet oiled fixative
2 tablespoons strawberry oiled fixative.

Combine all the ingredients and allow to mature. Once the pot pourri has been poured around the base of the tree, make sure that the top has a fair scattering of oak moss, pebbles and cones.

Pot pourri for the nursery

Pot pourri, with its bite-sized ingredients, must of course be kept well out of the reach of young children. Having said that, there is no reason why you couldn't make a suitable pot pourri and place it high up on a nursery shelf well away from inquisitive fingers! The main beneficial effect that herbs could have on a baby or small child would be to help him or her sleep, so I have mainly dwelt on relaxing or sleep-inducing mixtures for this section.

Hop nod

This funny name came about when we tried mixing sleeping hops with the Land of Nod, and it just stuck! Hops have long been known for their sleep-inducing qualities, and even if this pot pourri doesn't manage to send anyone to sleep it still smells lovely.

6 cups hop flowers
1 cup cracked nutmegs
3 cups red clover flower heads
1 cup chopped orange peel
2 cups small heather sprigs
2 tablespoons sweet orange oiled fixative
3 tablespoons geranium oiled fixative
2 tablespoons nutmeg oiled fixative
4 tablespoons rose oiled fixative

Combine all the ingredients and allow to mature. To display the pot pourri, why not line a small doll's crib or Moses basket with fabric, fill it with the pot pourri and decorate with ribbons.

Sleepy lullaby

This is another herbal mixture that is supposed to have a soporific effect. It's a traditional West Country mix that I am assured works wonders when stuffed into a small pillow, so maybe it will still be as effective when used as a pot pourri.

3 cups lavender flowers
3 cups spearmint leaves
2 cups sage leaves
2 cups dill leaves and flowers
1½ cups primrose flowers and leaves
4 tablespoons lavender oiled fixative
3 tablespoons peppermint oiled fixative
2 tablespoons camomile oiled fixative
1 tablespoon sage oiled fixative

Combine all the ingredients and allow to mature. To display this pot pourri, you can put it well out of reach of exploring fingers by hanging it from an overhead lampshade. If you choose a small hamper for the basket you could attach ribbon strings to it, then tie those ribbons to the lampshade. I found the easiest way was to make small holes in the lampshade and thread the ribbons through them. After lining the basket you can fill it with pot pourri and glue or wedge the lid open, or even remove it entirely. As a finishing touch, glue a tiny fluffy duck or bunny on the edge of the hamper; the overall effect will be one of a hot air balloon with a basket and passenger! It will appeal to the under-fives – I know, because it has been well and truly road-tested!

A soft pot pourri to help a baby sleep can be put well out of reach in the nursery.

Topiary trees are a beautiful way to arrange dried flowers, and here the base has been filled with pot pourri to give an added feature to the display.

BATHROOM POT POURRI

One of the most popular rooms in the house for bowls of pot pourri is the bathroom. The heat and steam produced whenever you have a bath helps to bring out the scent of the pot pourri, and there are many recipes that would work well for the bathroom. Some people may want a colour co-ordinated recipe to tone with the colour of their bathroom, while others might want to follow through the watery theme. The other recipe I have included in this bathroom section is a soft peachy blend to help you relax, whether you're taking a long relaxing bath or a quick shower.

Blue moon
The name of this pot pourri is in no way connected with how rarely the family gives you a chance to have a long relaxing bath; it is supposed to refer to the colour!

2 cups cornflowers
2 cups blue mallow flowers
2 cups lavender flowers
4 cups blue hydrangea florets
1 cup pearl beads
1 cup juniper berries
2 tablespoons lavender oiled fixative
1 tablespoon lemon oiled fixative
2 tablespoons ylang-ylang oiled fixative
2 tablespoons rosewood oiled fixative
2 tablespoons violet oiled fixative

Combine all the ingredients and allow to mature. To display, place in a large deep glass bowl, perhaps with a faint blue/green tinge to the glass. Then decorate with pressed blue flowers, such as borage, larkspur and hydrangeas. Having filled the bowl with the pot pourri, slide the pressed flowers down between the pot pourri and the sides of the bowl. Then add some silica dried flowers to the top of the bowl, making sure that a reasonable number of the pearl beads are visible on the surface.

Peach panache
3 cups peach rose petals ('Gerda' dry to a good colour)
3 cups pink rose-buds
3 cups 'Cheerfulness' narcissus
1 cup broken cinnamon sticks
1/2 cup chopped vanilla pods
1 cup orange or tangerine peel strips
6 tablespoons peach oiled fixative
2 tablespoons rose oiled fixative
1 tablespoon cinnamon oiled fixative
1 tablespoon vanilla oiled fixative
2 tablespoons sweet orange oiled fixative

Combine all the ingredients well and allow to mature. To display, fill a large dark-coloured basket with a handle. Decorate the handle and edge of the basket with silica dried orange, peach or cherry blossoms and tiny dried kumquats. Between the flowers and the fruit, glue some dried or glycerined leaves and narrow peach-coloured ribbons.

Watery nocturne

2 cups love-in-a-mist (Nigella) *flowers*
2 cups eucalyptus leaves
2 cups raspberry leaves
2 cups cream rose petals
2 cups 'Paper White' narcissus
1/2 cup peeled ginger root
1 cup small pearly shells
1/2 cup pieces of liquorice root
3 tablespoons musk rose oiled fixative
2 tablespoons geranium oiled fixative
2 tablespoons raspberry oiled fixative
1 tablespoon patchouli oiled fixative
2 tablespoons lavender oiled fixative

Combine all the ingredients and allow to mature. To display, place in a large shallow blue bowl and decorate with small starfish or sea urchin shells.

CHAPTER SIX

Simmering Pot Pourri and Mixtures Without Fixatives

Although simmering or stove top pot pourri is very popular in the USA it is not as well-known in Europe. In this style of pot pourri rather more robust botanicals are mixed with essential oils and fixative and then simmered in water over a heat source.

You can buy purpose-built steamers which use candle power or those powered by electricity. Simmering pot pourri can also be placed in an old saucepan and simmered on a wood-burning stove, cooker hob or hot plate. You can choose to make your kitchen smell of traditional baking aromas or to fill your bedroom with the scent of gardenias and orange blossom. The choice is yours.

Also covered in this chapter are a selection of recipes using cones and seed pods that will absorb the essential oils, so that there is no need for orris root or other fixatives. This can be useful if you have difficulty getting hold of orris root at any time or just want to try another type of pot pourri. The cone mixes are particularly suitable for Christmas and other festive recipes.

Simmering pot pourri burners create a strong and immediate fragrance in any part of the house, as and when you need it.

SIMMERING POT POURRI

Stove top pot pourri is fun to make. It has a slightly different method to that of the normal dry pot pourri, but that just adds to the interest. Originally designed for use on wood-burning stoves, simmering pot pourri can be very useful for giving an instant burst of fragrance just before guests arrive or for camouflaging a lingering smell that you want to banish. I find the results very uplifting, and scenting the room with mulled wine smells, summer berries or other delights can make me feel really good. If you use a saucepan to simmer the pot pourri in water on top of the cooker, always use the same pan and keep it purely for that purpose!

You can reuse the pot pourri mix two or three times, depending on how long it simmered and how strong the mixture was in the first place. It is important to strain the botanicals and allow them to dry thoroughly when you are not using them, otherwise they will go mouldy. They also need to be kept out of children's reach in case they are believed to be edible.

One way of using this pot pourri is to package it in small bundles that can easily be fished out of the water to dry. The look of this pot pourri is totally irrelevant, in the same way as the original moist pot pourri was made to be hidden in a jar. With this type, the scent is everything!

When you are concocting these mixtures the important factor to remember is whether you like the smell of the ingredient or not. There is no point in including flower petals as they generally do not impart a particularly strong perfume, with the exception perhaps of rose petals or any other strongly scented flowers. You will need more robust items such as seeds and leaves, which will release their smells to some extent, but these will be boosted by the presence of essential oils and their fixatives.

Suitable ingredients
You will need to prepare your oiled fixative mixtures in the same way as for the dry pot pourri (see page 51) and allow them to mature for a couple of days or so before you use them. The choice of ingredients is probably not as wide as for other types of pot pourri, but there are still many plants and herbs to choose from. I have listed those which I use most frequently and you can experiment with any others that come to mind.

Herbs and leaves
Basil, bay, eucalyptus, lemon balm, lemon thyme, lemon verbena, various mints, rosemary, rue, sage and thyme.

Fruits and berries
Orange peel, lemon, grapefruit, mango, tangerine, kumquats, limes, apple pieces, peach pieces, juniper berries, elderberries, pear slices, dried banana chips, coconut and vanilla pods.

Spices and woods
Allspice, star anise, caraway, cardamom, cedar chips, cinnamon sticks,

cloves, coriander, fennel seeds, ginger root, nutmeg pieces, sandalwood and liquorice root.

I also use lavender flowers, rose-buds (scented roses only) and oak moss.

Choosing the fixative

You will need less oiled fixative mix than that used for dry pot pourri as the heat produced when the ingredients are simmered makes them all work much harder. Ingredients such as cloves and cinnamon give out a much stronger perfume when they are heated than when they are included cold in a normal pot pourri recipe. Although orris root is becoming increasingly expensive as it gains in popularity for pot pourri manufacture, calamus root is not suitable for simmering pot pourri work as it gives off an unpleasant earthy smell. An alternative is to use dried and chopped orange peel to soak up the essential oils, although I would not recommend this as an alternative for a long-lasting dry pot pourri. However, if you are only going to be able to use this simmering mixture one or twice, its cost must come into the equation somewhere.

Making simmering pot pourri

The method for these recipes is very similar to that for the dry pot pourri. Pre-mix the oil and fixative or oil and chopped orange peel mixtures and let them stand in separate jam jars for a couple of days to mature. When they are ready, choose your group of ingredients and mix them with the oiled fixative, then leave the whole mixture in a sealed and labelled container to age or mature for about two or three weeks.

Once it is ready to use you can package it in small calico bundles. Cut out 9 in (22.5 cm) in diameter circles of calico, put a couple of tablespoons of the mixture in the centre, gather up the edges and tie with a ribbon.

This could be in a suitable colour – red or green for Christmassy smells, orange ribbon for citrus mixtures, pink for rose mixes, and so on. These bundles should then be kept in air-tight jars or containers until you want to use them. If you are giving them as a gift, write a label listing the ingredients and the instructions for use.

Mulled cider pot pourri

1 cup chopped dry apple slices
1 cup allspice berries
1 cup broken cinnamon sticks
1 cup whole cloves
1 cup dry orange peel soaked in 2 teaspoons apple oil and 1 teaspoon allspice oil

Combine the ingredients and leave to mature. This recipe makes enough for about 30 bundles and looks very attractive packed in red calico bundles and tied with green ribbon. It makes a delightful gift when packed with a mixture of flavours, each one in a different fabric and piled high in a basket.

Cones look stunning, heaped in a basket beside the fire. If you fragrance them with a few drops of oil they will give out a subtle perfume both before they go on the fire and while they are burning.

French château

2 cups lavender flowers
2 cups scented rose-buds
1 cup chopped vanilla pods
1 cup mixed herbs

1 cup orris root soaked in 1 teaspoon
lavender oil, 1 teaspoon rose oil and
½ teaspoon vanilla oil

Combine the ingredients and leave to mature. This mixture is good packaged in calico or linen bundles. If they are intended as a gift, you could pack some bundles with a card listing the ingredients and explaining the uses and tuck in some small bundles of lavender tied with ribbons to match.

Strawberry and orange preserve

2 cups chopped orange peel
2 cups rose hips
½ cup black peppercorns
1 cup white peppercorns
1 cup strawberry leaves

1 cup orris root soaked in 2 teaspoons
strawberry oil, 1 teaspoon sweet
orange oil and a few drops black
pepper oil

Combine all the ingredients and leave to mature. To package as a gift, tie into small pink bundles with pink ribbon. Tie on a gift card with a strawberry stencilled on to the front and full instructions inside.

Celebration flowers

This mix contains herbs and oils to celebrate any special occasion.

2 cups oak moss
2 cups chopped grapefruit peel
2 cups scented rose-buds
1 cup hibiscus flowers

1 cup orris root soaked in 1 teaspoon
gardenia oil, 1 teaspoon rose oil, 1
teaspoon neroli oil and 1 teaspoon
jasmine oil

Combine all the ingredients and leave to mature. To package, particularly if they are being made as a special anniversary gift or a wedding present, wrap the bundles in satin lining material and tie with narrow lace.

Rudolph's choice

The most popular time of year to use a simmering pot pourri is Christmas, to welcome guests. This collection of ingredients creates a lovely festive aroma that quickly pervades the house and cheers the heart!

2 cups pine or spruce needles
1 cup broken cinnamon sticks
2 cups chopped orange peel
1 cup rose-buds
½ cup cloves
½ cup allspice berries

1½ cups orris root soaked in 2
teaspoons cranberry oil, 1 teaspoon
pine oil, 1 teaspoon sweet orange oil
and 1 teaspoon cinnamon oil

Combine all the ingredients and leave to mature. Make up into little bundles using a fabric printed with Christmas trees or other festive motifs. Tie with red and green ribbons and package in a decorated basket.

DRY POT POURRI RECIPES WITHOUT FIXATIVES

Dried cones, seed pods and woods are included in these recipes as an alternative to orris or calamus roots that are usually used to fix the main perfume. The look of cones somewhat restricts you to autumn and wintery themes, but seed pods or woods can also be used to good effect and can offer more scope. The essential oils are sprayed (if the oils you have bought come in an atomiser – do not try filling your own atomiser as this is too wasteful) or dropped on to the cones, seeds or woods. The mixture will benefit from being aged in a sealed container for a couple of weeks.

Possible cones, seed pods and woods
All the following are suitable: *pine cones, larch cones, eucalyptus fruits, bakuli fruits, cypress, and any other small fir cones, senna pods, costus flowers (like mini pine cones), hibiscus, cedar wood, sandalwood, quassia chips, most tree bark, cinnamon and in desperation balsa wood shavings!*

In all cases, soak the woods, cones or seeds before mixing them with the other ingredients and, if possible, leave the mixture in a sealed bag or box for a couple of weeks. If this is not possible, or you are just too impatient, you can display it immediately. The scent may change slightly over the first couple of weeks but I would suggest using fairly straightforward blends of perfume for this type of recipe anyway. This is also a good way to use ready-blended perfume oils or oils sold to refresh commercial pot pourri mixes. I am not promising the depth and longevity of other methods, but it is quick and easy! If the fragrance starts to fade then just re-oil the cones or whichever ingredient held the oil in the first place.

Fireside fragrance
A collection of pine cones collected in a nearby wood can be transformed by dropping a different choice of essential oil on to several groups of them and then combining them all in a large basket and placing them on the hearth.

Large basket of cones, mixed shapes and sizes
Selection of perfume oils or essential oils, for example sweet orange, bayberry, cinnamon, spicy rose and apple

Fill the basket you want to use and then divide the cones into five groups. Scent the cones in group one with the sweet orange oil, group two with bayberry, and so on. I usually allow about six drops of oil for small cones but obviously you will have to allow nearer twenty drops for large ones.

When the cones have been re-oiled several times, or you are just plain fed up with them, they will burn beautifully on the fire and give out a lovely perfume as their final performance!

If you are giving a selection of the scented cones as a Christmas present, then choose a basket which will suit the recipient's hearth, and decorate it with beautiful tartan bows on each end of the handles and perhaps a few bundles of cinnamon sticks tied with gold cord.

Woodland magic

A mixture of woods and spices, roots and nuts combine to give a magic aroma of mossy walks and crunchy leaves.

1 cup small pine cones
2 cups oak moss
1 cup sandalwood
1 cup quassia chips
1 cup pine needles
1 cup lemon grass rings
1 cup cedarwood

1 cup cinnamon sticks
1/2 cup cloves
1/2 cup whole star anise
1 cup costus flowers soaked in 1
 teaspoon pine oil, 1 teaspoon spiced
 orange oil, 2 teaspooons allspice oil
 and 2 teaspoons violet oil

Mix all the ingredients, place in a polythene bag and seal for two weeks. Alternatively, you can cheat and display the mix immediately.

Eastern promise

1 cup sandalwood chips
1 cup cedar chips
1 cup broken cinnamon sticks
1 cup cracked nutmegs
1/2 cup cardamom pods
1 cup star anise
1 cup chopped vanilla pods
1 cup small pieces ginger root

1/2 cup whole cloves
1 cup chopped lemon peel
1 cup orange peel soaked in 1 teaspoon
 ylang-ylang oil, 1 teaspoon patchouli
 oil, 1 teaspoon frankincense oil, 2
 teaspoons cinnamon oil, 1 teaspoon
 neroli oil

Treat the ingredients as for 'Woodland Magic'.

Peach brandy pot pourri

2 cups dried apple or peach slices
2 cups cream or apricot globe amaranth
 flowers
2 cups chopped cinnamon sticks
2 cups nutmeg pieces
2 cups peach roses – buds or petals

2 cups hibiscus flowers
2 cups chopped orange peel soaked in 4
 teaspoons any peach essential oil, 1
 teaspoon cinnamon oil, 2 teaspoons
 brandy essence and 1 teaspoon
 vanilla oil

Treat as above, but this mixture really does benefit from being allowed to mature.

OTHER IDEAS FOR PINE CONES AND FLOWERS

Pine cones and other absorbent materials can also be oiled and then used in decorative arrangements. Wreaths with fragrant pine cones or pieces of oiled cinnamon or ginger root can give a room a lovely perfume. The essential oils can also be dropped on to the centre of dried flowers to scent a dried flower arrangement. You can either match the oil to the flower, dropping lavender on to a sprig of lavender, rose oil on to a rose, and so on, or a blended perfume oil can be dropped or sprayed over the entire arrangement to add a pleasant fragrance to the air.

CHAPTER SEVEN

Captive Fragrance

Althouth pot pourri is regaining its popularity as a room freshener and
source of fragrance, the use of sachets and scented cushions and pillows
never waned. Nothing can beat the subtle fragrance of a drawer filled
with lingerie and some perfumed sachets tucked away here and there –
it smells so luxurious!

There are a great many different uses all over the house for cushions,
pillows, sachets and pomanders. In this chapter I will be describing
how to make the scented mixtures to fill the pillows and other items.
There are also instructions on how to make various items for yourself or
as gifts. Don't worry if you hate sewing because there are ideas for
those who (like me!) have a panic attack when they see an electric
sewing machine. So everyone should find something in this chapter to
make their houses and cupboards smell sweeter than ever.

**Many kinds of cushions can be stuffed with herbs, or have a small pocket of
pot pourri sewn into the cover to give a gentle fragrance to the drawing
room, bedroom or anywhere else in the house.**

POT POURRI FOR CUSHIONS AND SACHETS

The recipes for making pot pourri fillings are quite different from those used for display, because the only factor that really matters in this case is the perfume. The mixture will, of course, be completely invisible unless you intend to use net or some other transparent fabric for the casing. This is possible and will be dealt with later in the chapter. The majority of the recipes and instructions, however, are written with the assumption that you will be filling sachets, made from opaque fabric.

Bulky sachets can be a problem in some settings, such as linen cupboards. Here you need slim, flat sachets that will tuck unobtrusively between sheets and blankets or duvets and their covers. When making sachets for use in the living room or bedroom it is still an advantage to have a moderately flat pillow as it is less likely to be knocked or damaged and it will tuck away in a corner without getting in the way.

Suitable fabrics
There is no limit to the types of materials that you could use to make your pillows and sachets, the only consideration being comfort and appearance. You could make a heavy tweed sachet if you really wish, but it would be better to find a medium-weight tweed as the more closely woven fabrics do not allow the fragrance to circulate as efficiently. The best fabrics for this type of work are light thin materials that will allow the gentle fragrances to be released. My favourite has to be silk, but it is a rather expensive fabric and there are many other suitable materials at far lower prices.

Suitable patterns
If the pillow or sachet is destined for a kitchen then gingham or plaid works well in a cotton or similarly lightweight fabric. All the small patterned flowery fabrics work beautifully. The size of the pattern must be in proportion to the size of the pillow. If the pattern repeat is enormous, then making a small sachet from that fabric will result in a sachet with half a flower in one corner and nothing else, or a tiny proportion of the pattern being seen. Choose a material with a tiny pattern and you will fit several pattern repeats on to each pillow, which will look much better.

Trimmings
Sachets for the bedroom look lovely trimmed with lace, embroidery or other embellishments. A large sweet bag (the old-fashioned name for a scented sachet) could be made up in a cotton furnishing fabric to match or tone with the curtains or chairs.

Sachets for all the family
Smelling nice is not the sole province of ladies, of course, and there are several recipes that are suitable for gentlemen. I have included some suggestions for 'his and hers' recipes for sachets, which make an unusual

present. The family pets can often benefit from herbal fragrances too. Cats, it is well known, love catnip, so maybe you could make your favourite feline a small sachet shaped like a mouse containing a catnip mixture. I can't guarantee how long it would last; on previous showing my cat managed to 'kill' the mouse very quickly and efficiently, but at least she had a lot of fun doing it!

Another idea for the pet section is to carry through the anti-moth and insect repellent properties of herbs by making a flea deterrent sachet for the dog's bed. There are several herbs that fleas hate, such as rue, camomile and pennyroyal, so you could mix them up and make a flat sachet for the bed. Knowing my dog she would eat it, but it's worth a try!

Using up old pot pourri mixtures
The most effective way to use pot pourri mixes in sachets is to powder the contents or to make a powdery mixture in the first place. Large beautiful and showy dried items have no place in this chapter; save them for your open bowls of fragrance. Making pillows can be a very good way to use up old or faded pot pourri, because by mixing it with an oiled fixative such as powdered orris root, it is brought back to life again. For a strong-smelling, long-lasting pillow, it is necessary to use a mix which is 50 per cent naturally scented botanical items and 50 per cent oiled fixative. You can use a smaller percentage of fixative but the sachet's fragrance will fade very much quicker.

Powdered mixtures
When the recipe calls for the mixture to be powdered, this can be done in a coffee grinder or blender, but do take the greatest care in rinsing out any grinding equipment that you have used very thoroughly afterwards. If you have ever tasted the delicious blend of Brazilian coffee and moth repellent pot pourri you'll realize why! I have an old blender/coffee grinder that I keep specifically for such anti-social uses as grinding pot pourri – actually, it's the one that produced the Brazilian and moth repellent coffee blend, because we never felt the same way about it ever again! If you do not have access to this type of equipment, all is not lost because you can either use a pestle and mortar or place all the ingredients in a sturdy polythene bag, fasten it securely and break down the contents with a rolling pin. This method can be excellent for venting frustration after a really bad day – just be careful if you get too rough with the mixture that you don't puncture the polythene bag!

Using up leftovers
You may well be a compulsive hoarder of fabric, lace, ribbons and other 'useful' bits, like me. Somehow the interest in pot pourri seems to attract people with squirrel-like tendencies! Now you can begin to collect suitable natural bits and pieces for your pot pourri work as well. Never throw away small leftover amounts of a particular blend of a pot pourri, although you shouldn't fill the display container so full that you are constantly having to clear up the spillage when it's out on display. Keep small quantities in sealed

polythene bags, the type with zip lock tops are excellent. When you are making a gift of a particular pot pourri, make up your main display and then make some small sachets in the same blend to use up the leftovers and to complete the present. If it is a gift for a bathroom, perhaps you could make some lacy sachets to hang with the towels, for a kitchen you could make some gingham bundles to hang in the cupboards, and so on.

Reviving old sachets

To revive old and tired sachets or mixes of pot pourri, one is often recommend to use brandy. Personally I would rather drink the brandy and use something else! Seriously, though, brandy works very well for the traditional moist pot pourri mentioned in Chapter One, but not so well on dry pot pourri or sachets. I would suggest that you add more essential oils to your mix instead. This entails removing the mixture from the bag and distributing the new essential oil evenly among the bulk.

However, as you have to empty the cushion or sachet to do this, can I suggest that it might be easier to use new, strongly fragranced pot pourri to refill the sachet as this will last far longer than the original mixture pepped up with new essential oils.

RECIPES FOR POWDERED POT POURRI

These mixtures are excellent for stuffing pillows, cushions and sachets but are totally unsuitable for display in an open bowl as the powder can easily be blown around by sudden gusts of wind.

Traditional Elizabethan sweet bag recipe

This recipe is taken from Sir Hugh Platt's book *Delights for Ladies*, published in 1594.

To Make an especial Sweet Powder for Sweet Bags
Take of Red and Damask Rose-leaves of each two ounces, of the purest Orris one pound, of Cloves three drams, Coriander seed one dram, Cyprus and Calamus of each halfe an ounce, Benzoin and the Storax of each three drams; beat them all save the Benzoin and the Storax and powder them by themselves, then take of Muske and Civet, of each twentie graines, mix these with a little of the foresaid powder with a warm Pestle, and so little by little you may mix it with all the rest, and so with Rose leaves dried you may put it up into your Sweet Bags and so keepe them seven yeares.

It is fascinating to research all the old original recipes; the recipe above was

Pretty sachets, or sweet bags as they were called, have been popular for many hundreds of years and add a special perfume to drawers and cupboards.

changed very little by the writers who followed. In 1625 Gervase Markham wrote *The English Housewife*, and his sweet bag recipe is not dissimilar except he mentions marjoram. He also recommends that the mixture is put into a taffety (taffeta) bag. Mary Dogget in *Her Book of Receipts*, written in 1682, changes the recipe slightly by adding dried lemon peel and oranges stuck with cloves. She claims that the recipe will be fine for a couple of years (perhaps the original recipe's boast of seven years was rather on the optimistic side!) So a hundred years later little had changed.

Moving on another hundred years, Mrs Glasse published *The Art of Cookery* in 1784 and included a recipe for sweet scented bags to lay with linen. This recipe includes white loaf sugar, and most of the ingredients are still easily obtainable today, so I feel it's worth quoting here.

Sweet scented bags to lay with linen

Eight ounces of damask rose leaves, eight ounces of coriander seeds, eight ounces of sweet orris root, eight ounces of Calamus aromaticus, *one ounce of mace, one ounce of cinnamon, half an ounce of cloves, four drachms of musk powder, two drachms of white loaf sugar, three ounces of lavender flowers and some of Rhodium wood. Beat them well together and make them in small silk bags.*

When I experimented with this recipe I modified it slightly. Damask rose petals (they referred to the petals as leaves in those days) were not available at the time, so I substituted commercially bought roses with essential oil added. Coriander, orris root, calamus root, mace, cinnamon and cloves were all to hand. I would never use musk powder because it's animal-based, so I used a musk essential oil that is synthetically produced. For four drachms use ½ oz (12 g), and for two drachms of white sugar, use ¼ oz (6 g). I substituted sandalwood for the rhodium wood because it was already here. The recipe is excellent and I would thoroughly recommend it. I made up several quantities of the mixture and filled antique silk and lace sachets with it to give as presents. To package the presents, I included a calligraphed version of the recipe with the book title and date.

The only other historical recipe for scented sachets that I have found to be really practical is one from *The Toilet of Flora*, published in 1775. Apart from the enjoyment of the scented cushions and sachets I get a great deal of satisfaction from producing something traditional that our ancestors were making some two and a half centuries ago.

Bags to scent linen

Take Rose leaves dried in the shade, Cloves beat to a gross powder and Mace scraped; mix them together, and put the composition into little bags.

This is a very simple recipe with no quantities but it is very quick and easy to make. I used one tablespoon of cloves and one of mace to every cup of dried rose petals. Again, I only had unscented petals so I added a little essential oil to them before putting them into the mixture.

Let us move on from these traditional recipes to some up-to-date versions, all of which smell lovely. Perhaps you should make them all and then choose where to position each fragrance!

Romantic orange blossom

1 cup orange blossom
1 cup rose petals
2 cups cut calamus root or orris root
3 teaspoons neroli oil
1 teaspoon rose oil
1 teaspoon allspice oil
1 teaspoon voilet oil

Use the same method as for dry pot pourri – mix the oils with the orris or calamus root and leave to mature in a jam jar for a couple of days. Once the oiled fixative is ready you can mix it with all the other ingredients. Place in a blender or grinder and process until it is a coarse powder. You can then mature the whole mix in a sealed polythene bag for a couple of weeks before you use it, or you can put it into the sachets immediately if you prefer.

Herbal mist

1 cup rosemary leaves
1 cup mint leaves
1/2 cup sage leaves
1/2 cup bay leaves
2 cups cut calamus or orris root
1 teaspoon rosemary oil
1 teaspoon peppermint oil
1 teaspoon basil oil
1 teaspoon marjoram oil
1 teaspoon sage oil
1 teaspoon thyme oil

Soak the calamus or orris root in the oils in the usual way, then mix all the ingredients and grind to a coarse powder.

Lemon sparkle

1 cup dried lemon peel
1 cup lemon verbena leaves
1/2 cup lemon balm and lemon thyme
1 cup cut orris or calamus root
2 teaspoons sweet orange oil
4 teaspoons lemon oil

Follow the method for making dry pot pourri, then grind to a coarse powder.

Allspice bouquet

1 cup allspice berries
1 cup cinnamon pieces
1/2 cup vanilla pods
1/2 cup carnation petals
1 cup cut calamus or orris root
3 teaspoons allspice oil
1 teaspoon vanilla oil
1 teaspoon cinnamon oil
1 teaspoon carnation oil

Follow the method given for making dry pot pourri, then grind to a coarse powder.

Woodland fantasy

1/2 cup cedar wood chips
1/2 cup sandalwood chips
1 cup oak moss
1/2 cup eucalyptus leaves
1 cup cut orris root or calamus root
1 teaspoon cedar oil
1 teaspoon pine needle oil
1 teaspoon sandalwood oil
1 teaspoon cinnamon oil
1 teaspoon violet oil
1 teaspoon patchouli oil

Follow the method given for making dry pot pourri, then grind to a coarse powder.

Lilac love

1 cup rose petals
1 cup lilac blossom
1/2 cup raspberry leaves
1/2 cup lemon balm leaves
1 cup cut orris root or calamus root
3 teaspoons lilac oil
2 teaspoons rose oil
1 teaspoon violet oil

Follow the method given for making dry pot pourri, then grind to a coarse powder.

Hop pillows have long been a popular answer to insomnia and herbal mixtures can also relax and promote sweet dreams!

MAKING A PERFUMED SACHET

All these recipes are intended for strongly scented small sachets to hang in wardrobes or closets, tuck in drawers or use with towels and linens. Although being able to sew is an advantage, it is by no means essential.

A traditional perfumed sachet for lingerie

Choose a suitable fabric. My favourite is real silk, but a pretty cotton, lawn or calico is just as suitable. If you want to fill the sachet with something pretty like lavender then you could choose a transparent fabric or layers of net. However, such materials are not suitable for powdered mixtures, so leave the ingredients whole.

Cut out two pieces of fabric 6 × 4 in (15 × 10 cm) and place them right sides together. Sew along three sides and then turn the bag right sides out. Using a funnel, fill the bag half to two-thirds full with your choice of pot pourri. Fold in the edges of the fourth side and oversew them to close the bag. You can then trim the sachet with lace, pearls, beads, ribbon roses or any other decoration you prefer.

A hanging sachet for a wardrobe or cupboad

As an alternative you can make a hanging sachet. Cut out two pieces of fabric 8 × 6 in (20 × 15 cm), place them right sides together, and sew along one of the shorter sides and the two longer sides. Half to two-thirds fill the sachet with pot pourri, using a funnel. Then secure the bag with a ribbon tied a third of the way down. Lace can then be attached to the top of the bag or around the edge. Attach a long loop of ribbon to the back of the sachet so it can be hung up.

An alternative idea for the hanging sachet is to make two smaller ones and link them with a single length of ribbon, about 18 in (45 cm) long. The pair of sachets can then be hung over a hanger in a wardrobe, over a hook on the back of a door, or even over a doorknob.

HERBAL AND SLEEP PILLOWS

These herbal pillows have been made for many years and probably derived from the original straw and fragrant grass mattresses. They became extremely popular in Victorian times and are a charming way to soothe yourself to sleep.

The mixtures are totally different to those given for the perfumed sachets on the previous pages. If you used a pillow with such strong-smelling ingredients as those you would probably spend all night sneezing; because a herbal or sleep pillow is placed very near your face, it must have a much more subtle fragrance.

I usually make the pillow about 12 × 10 in (30 × 25 cm). You can use any fabric you like, but bear in mind that it is usual to place the little herb pillow inside the standard pillow case, so it is often unseen. Comfort is of paramount importance; even if the hops or herbal mixture makes you drowsy you won't be able to sleep if the pillow is desperately uncomfortable!

Make a calico or muslin inner bag first to hold the herbs. Then make another bag of wadding (as used in quilting), choosing a medium thickness, and place the inner bag in that. Finally cover that with a washable cover; cotton, linen and lawn all work well.

Here is a selection of sleepytime remedies!

Hypnotic herbal mix

1/2 cup rosemary leaves
1/2 cup any variety of thyme
1/2 cup mint leaves
1/2 cup catnip (don't tell your cat)
1/2 cup camomile flowers
1/4 cup cut calamus root
1/2 teaspoon rosemary oil
1/2 teaspoon mint oil

Soak the calamus root in the two types of oil and allow it to mature for a couple of days in a sealed jam jar. Then mix all the ingredients together and grind them in a blender or coffee grinder to a powder. Use to fill one pillow.

Golden slumbers

1/2 cup elderflowers
1/2 cup cowslips or primroses
2 tablespoons nutmeg
1/2 cup golden rose petals
1/2 cup orange peel
1/4 cup cut orris or calamus root
1/2 teaspoon nutmeg oil
1 teaspoon rose oil
1 teaspoon neroli oil

Soak the calamus or orris root in the oils and store in a sealed jam jar for a couple of days. Then powder all the ingredients in a blender or grinder.

Sleepytime hops

2 1/2 cups hop flowers
1 cup heather
1 tablespoon calamus or orris root
1/4 teaspoon nutmeg oil

In this recipe the first two ingredients can be used alone without the need for the oil and fixative. Just fill the pillow with the flowers, making sure there are no sharp pieces of heather to make the pillow uncomfortable. Alternatively, soak the calamus or orris root in the nutmeg oil and store in a closed jam jar for two days. Then grind to a coarse powder.

Minted lavender lullaby

1 cup lavender flowers
½ cup mint leaves
½ cup scented geranium leaves
½ cup lemon verbena leaves
¼ cup calamus or orris root
¼ teaspoon mint oil
¼ teaspoon geranium oil
¼ teaspoon lemon verbena oil
¼ teaspoon lavender oil

Soak the calamus or orris root in the oils. Store in a closed jam jar for two days to mature. Then mix all the ingredients together and grind to a coarse power in either a blender or a coffee grinder.

SCENTED SACHETS IN MATCHING PAIRS

As an amusing and unusual gift, why not make a pair of sachets for a couple, starting with the same perfumed base and then making slight alterations to suit the individual. A basic herbal mix, for example, could have some woody notes added for a man and some floral notes added for a woman. Here are some suggestions to start you thinking.

Titania and Oberon

This is a delicious mix of sweet grass and hay smells, with some delicate woodland fragrances added for the man's sachet and some wild flower fragrances for the woman's.

½ cup camomile flowers
½ cup red clover flowers
½ cup hops
½ cup rue leaves
½ cup silver artemisia leaves
½ cup cut calamus or orris root
1 teaspoon violet oil

Soak the calamus or orris root with the violet oil and leave for two days in a sealed jam jar. Mix all the ingredients together and divide in half. To the masculine half, add ½ cup oak moss, ½ cup violet leaves and ¼ cup orris or calamus root that has been soaked with ½ teaspoon of cedar wood oil. To the more feminine half add ½ cup elder flowers, ½ cup rose petals and ¼ cup orris or calamus root that has been soaked with ½ teaspoon of lily of the valley oil. Seal and label each polythene bag and check them after two weeks, then powder the ingredients and fill the sachets.

Anti-moth mixtures are easily concocted and seem very effective, without smelling as unpleasant as old-fashioned moth balls.

Morning bells and evening pillows

This pair of sachets has a shared base of soft fruity scents. The morning sachet contains some more invigorating, wake-up ingredients, while the evening sachet includes more soporific soothing herbs.

½ cup lemon peel
½ cup raspberry leaves
½ cup strawberry leaves
½ cup apple pieces
½ cup jasmine flowers
½ cup lemon scented geranium leaves
½ cup cut orris root
¼ teaspoon apple oil
¼ teaspoon pear oil
¼ teaspoon strawberry oil
¼ teaspoon sweet orange oil

Soak the orris or calamus root in the four oils and store in a sealed jar for two days. Then mix with all the other ingredients and divide in half into two polythene bags. To the Morning Bells half add ½ cup mint leaves, ½ cup coriander seeds, ¼ cup fennel seeds and ½ cup dried grapefruit peel soaked in ½ teaspoon bergamot oil.

To the Evening Pillows half add ½ cup hop flowers, ½ cup lavender and ½ cup rhubarb root soaked in 1 teaspoon geranium oil.

Seal and label the two bags and leave to mature for two weeks. Once they are ready check the fragrances and if you are happy with them then powder and package into sachets.

PROTECTING CLOTHES AND LINEN FROM MOTHS

Moths seem to have been a perennial problem for at least the last four hundred or five hundred years. I uncovered some wonderful quotes while looking for inspiration among the old herbal books.

Bankes' Herbal, published 1525:

Rosemary: Also take the flowres and put them in a chest amonge your clothes or amonge bookes and moughtes shall not hurte them.

They seem much fiercer creatures spelt that way rather than plain moths, don't you think?

Lavender, santolina or cotton lavender, artemisia and wormwood are all excellent moth deterrents and even good against 'dirty, filthy beasts' as one writer puts it. The mind boggles! Many herbs and spices can be used to sweeten linen and protect your clothes, either singly or mixed together.

Mothaway
1 cup scented geranium leaves
½ cup orange peel
½ cup lemon balm
½ cup whole cloves
1 cup silver artemisia or mugwort leaves
1 cup oak moss
½ cup cut orris root or calamus root
½ teaspoon clove oil
½ teaspoon geranium oil
½ teaspoon lavender oil

Soak the calamus or orris root with the essential oils and leave in a closed jam jar for two days to mature. Then mix all the other ingredients together and grind them coarsely in a blender or coffee grinder. Store in a polythene bag for two weeks so the mixture can mature and then put into sachets as required.

OUTDOOR POT POURRI

One of the most irritating parts of outdoor entertaining is the uninvited winged guests that usually turn up. Mosquitoes are one of my pet hates and probably not very popular with you either. I have developed this mixture to be both an insect deterrent generally, and a mosquito deterrent specifically. I would suggest that you make large sachets of this mix and join them in pairs with canvas or strong ribbons, then hang them over the arms or backs of your garden chairs. Do not lower yourself to using them as mosquito swatters as an over-enthusiastic guest of mine once did!

Mozzieoff
2 cups artemisia, wormwood or mugwort leaves
2 cups pyrethrum flowers
1 cup lavender flowers
1 cup anise hyssop flowers
1 cup rosemary
2 cups santolina or cotton lavender
2 cups cut orris root
1 fl oz (25 ml) citronella oil

Soak the orris root in the oil and store for two days in a closed jam jar. Then mix all the ingredients together and use to fill large sachets. Keep them in a sealed polythene bag when not in use.

CHAPTER EIGHT

Pot Pourri for Gifts

In this last chapter I have collected together all the slightly unusual
ideas that I use. When you are looking for inspiration for a present for
someone, it sometimes takes a new idea or two to help you decide what
to make.

The main link between all the ideas in this chapter is that I think they
are a delightful way to show you care, whether you are giving a present
to your hostess, family or friends. None of the ideas are difficult to
follow: they are all fairly straightforward and once you have begun
you'll be surprised at how easy it is to make your own fragranced gifts
for everyone. Be warned, however: the better you make them, the more
likely it is you will be inundated with requests from family and friends
. . . 'You couldn't make me one just the same, could you? . . .'

**A varied collection of scented wreaths which are easy to make
and fragrance with your collection of essential oils.**

POT POURRI PASTILLES

These are an alternative way to make your own pot pourri. They can either be tucked into drawers and closets or displayed with other pot pourri as a decorative feature. If you have very young children in the house I would not recommend them as they could be mistaken for something edible.

The easiest way to produce these pastilles is to mix gum tragacanth (available from a chemist or drugstore) with orris root and essential oils and treat it much like modelling clay. I have used a food mixer for this job but it's a little difficult to clean it up afterwards.

Cinnamon scented hearts
1 cup gum tragacanth
½ cup powdered cinnamon
½ cup powdered orris root or calamus root
1–1½ cups water
½ fl oz (12 ml) cinnamon oil

Mix together the cinnamon oil, the powdered orris or calamus root and the cinnamon. When they are well mixed add the gum tragacanth. Then add the water gradually, kneading well as though you were making bread. I would advise wearing household gloves unless you want to smell of cinnamon for ages afterwards! Alternatively, you can experiment with the food mixer, but do allow plenty of time to clean it afterwards.

When you have a firm dough, roll it out (using a rolling pin kept for this purpose only) and cut out heart shapes. Leave to set.

Rose drops
1 cup gum tragacanth
½ cup powdered dark red rose petals
½ cup powdered orris root or calamus root
1–1½ cups water
½ fl oz (12 ml) rose oil

Mix all the ingredients as for the cinnamon hearts but use a rose- or flower-shaped cutter. If you want to make the flowers a little darker in colour you can add a tiny amount of red food colouring.

Ginger cats
1 cup gum tragacanth
½ cut powdered ginger
½ cut powdered orris or calamus root
1–1½ cups water
½ fl oz (12 ml) ginger oil

Mix all the ingredients as for the cinnamon hearts. Use a cat-shaped cutter or another shape if you don't have a cat. You could add a little colouring if you want a brighter ginger cat!

Violet dragonflies

1 cup gum tragacanth
½ cup powdered violet leaves
½ cup powdered orris or calamus root
1–1½ cups water
½ fl oz (12 ml) violet oil

Mix the ingredients and roll out as for cinnamon hearts. Use any shaped cutter you like – there aren't many dragonflies around, I suppose, and the ones shown in the photograph were made with a cutter I bought in Japan. The pastilles would look just as pretty made into leaves, flowers or any other shape you happen to have.

SCENTED BEADS

Perfumed beads have been around for hundreds of years. They originated as rosary beads and were worn by people in Tudor times in the faint hope that they would provide protection from disease. The perfume can be very long lasting but these beads don't rate as desperately sophisticated jewellery. I would suggest hanging them over the bedpost or keeping them in a dish on your dressing table rather than wearing them.

The method is very similar to that for making pastilles, but it is more important that the beads should be of a uniform size. I use a tiny melon baller to make the beads but any small measure or teaspoon will do.

Sweet and spicy beads

1–2 oz (25–50 g) allspice berries
1 cup mixed spices such as cloves, cinnamon and nutmeg
½ cup gum tragacanth
½ teaspoon vanilla oil
½ teaspoon cinnamon oil
water to mix

Ignore the allspice berries for the time being but place all the other ingredients into an old blender or mixing bowl. Add the essential oils. Then add the water slowly until it forms a thick paste. Take up equal-sized portions of the mixture using a small scoop or part of a teaspoon until all the mixture is used up. Then roll the portions into complete balls, small cubes, small sausage shapes or whatever you wish. It is easier to do this if you have oiled your hands, either with some of the essential oil or, if you wish to diminish the amount your hands will smell, use vegetable oil instead. I tried wearing household gloves but they were too cumbersome for this recipe. The best way is to smother yourself in essential oil, produce wonderful smelling beads and put up with the fact that you will smell odd for a little while!

Once you have rolled the beads into shapes you should leave them to dry out for an hour or so. Arm yourself with strong thread or fine nylon filament

and a long needle. Then prepare the allspice berries. Place them in a pan of hot water (but don't let them boil) for about 4 or 5 minutes until they begin to soften, and drain. Now begin to thread up your beads. Thread the balls or cubes you have made with the vanilla spice mixture alternately with the allspice berries until you have a string of the length you require. Then tie the ends of the threads together and leave to dry out for at least 48 hours.

You could also add ceramic or wooden beads, glass or amber antique beads, ribbons or other accessories when you come to display them. Many other fragrances could be used, so don't feel limited to spicy combinations. Powdered rose petals and rose essential oils can be just as successful as herbal mixes, fruit and spice mixtures or any other choice.

SCENTED POMANDERS

Traditional fruit-based pomanders are fun to make and look very attractive piled into a fruit bowl or other container on a table. There is no limit as to which fruits you can use to make up the pomanders, from large grapefruit to tiny kumquats. It depends on your time, patience and the effect that you want.

I will give the instructions for an orange as that is about midway in the size range, so you can scale the ingredients up or down accordingly.

Sweet orange pomander

1 thick-skinned firm orange
2 oz (50 g) or more cloves
1 tablespoon powdered orris or calamus root
1 tablespoon mixed spice
few drops vanilla or sweet orange essential oil
wooden skewer

Pierce the fruit from one end to the other with the wooden skewer. This is left in place to provide a hole through which ribbons can be threaded once the pomander is finished. Then insert the whole cloves in the orange skin, using a small knitting needle or cocktail stick if the skin seems particularly tough. You will probably need a lot more cloves than you think as I find that many of them are broken in the packet and do not have any heads left. The broken pieces can all be used in pot pourri, so nothing will be wasted; be prepared and have enough cloves just in case. Nothing is more irritating than sitting down and starting a pomander only to find that you have run out of cloves!

Cover the surface of the orange with cloves in the most even pattern you

Scented pastilles can add a new dimension to a pot pourri mix and are as easy to make as playing with children's modelling dough.

can manage. I usually keep to simple straight lines as this is probably the easiest way. Once the orange is covered with cloves, mix the orris or calamus root with the mixed spice and put the spice mixture into a sturdy polythene bag.

Distribute a few drops of essential oil on to any visible pieces of orange skin, then put the orange into the polythene bag with the spice mixture. Roll it gently around in the mix until it is completely covered, then remove it and place in a paper bag in a warm, dry place, such as a cupboard or drawer, for three or four weeks. You can cheat and put it in a slow oven but I'm never very happy with the results.

There are several different powdered mixes in which to roll the pomander. The spicy mix is best known and will always be popular, but you can experiment and see whether you prefer one of the following combinations.

Violet, rose and musk pomander

This combination was used by Philbert Guibert in Paris in 1639.

Stud the orange with cloves and then drop some musk oil on to the skin between the cloves. Roll the orange in the following mixture:

½ cup powdered violet leaves
½ cup powdered orris root
½ cup powdered scented rose petals

Pomander of herbs

Use an apple instead of an orange and stud it completely with cloves. Then drop some apple oil on to the skin. Roll in the following mixture:

½ cup powdered mixed herbs
½ cup powdered calamus or orris root
½ cup powdered rosemary sprigs

Apple wreaths

Still on the subject of apples, dried apple slices can make a charming feature in a kitchen, hallway or anywhere else in the house. The use of dried apple and other fruit slices is much more prevalent in the USA than in Europe, but it's a custom that really ought to catch on here as we have an awful lot of apples in the autumn!

Choose red rosy apples as they give a better colour to the finished product.

3–4 large red rosy apples
juice of one lemon
1 tablespoon mixed spice
1 tablespoon powdered orris root
3–4 teaspoons cinnamon oil
7–8 in (17.5–20 cm) ring or sturdy wire with hanger
green or brown florists' tape
hot-glue gun and glue sticks
cinnamon sticks, ribbon and dried roses

Slice the apples in slices about ¼ in (6 mm) thick. Paint them with the lemon juice. Place them on a baking tray and dry in the bottom of the oven on the lowest setting, treating them as you would meringues. Once they are dry (this can take several hours, depending on the oven setting) remove them from the oven and drop some cinnamon oil on to them before they cool. Mix together the orris root and the mixed spice and sprinkle it lavishly on to the apple slices.

Once the slices have cooled, tap off any residual spice mix and, using the hot-glue gun, stick the slices around the wire ring, overlapping them as they go round. I'm sure it would be possible to use a strong tacky glue as an alternative, but you would have to work with the ring flat on the work surface and it would take far longer for the glue to dry.

Once the wreath is complete, decorate with the cinnamon sticks, ribbons and roses as shown in the photograph. Again, these should be attached with the hot glue gun. Similar wreaths could be made from apple peelings or smaller pieces of apple, pear or peach.

SCENTED STRAW HATS

Another attractive way to display pot pourri is to fill the crown of a straw hat with it and then cover it with a couple of layers of net. This keeps the pot pourri tidy but allows the perfume to waft around. The brim of the hat can then be decorated with ribbons and dried flowers in a colour scheme to please your taste or that of the recipient.

Ingredients for a straw hat
1 large straw hat
approximately 8 oz (225 g) pot pourri
wide ribbon
2 bunches dried roses
white Statice dumosa, *or sea lavender*
apricot Statice sinuata
pink larkspur
1 bunch Nigella *seed heads*
small bunch gypsophila
two pieces of net
wired pearls and narrow ribbon

Cut the two pieces of net into circles a little bigger than the depth of the crown of the hat. Using a toning cotton, tack the net with running stitches securely inside the crown of the hat, leaving enough room to pour in the pot pourri. This can be accomplished by making a cone out of a sheet of paper and pouring the pot pourri through it. Then attach the rest of the net on top.

Attach the wide ribbon around the brim of the hat and finish with a bow at the back. Then with a hot-glue gun (no other method gives such a perfect finish), attach the dried flowers. First arrange some sprays of white *Statice dumosa*, or sea lavender. Then remove all the leaves from the roses and cut down the stem length to about 2 in (5 cm). Glue the roses evenly all around the hat. Add the apricot *Statice sinuata*, larkspur and *Nigella* evenly around the brim.

Then attach the wired pearls and loops of narrow ribbon. Finally, fill in any obvious gaps with tiny sprays of gypsophila. Glue a loop of ribbon securely on to the back of the hat so you can hang it up. The hat could either be hung on the wall or over a hook away from the wall to allow the pot pourri fragrance to circulate more freely.

The same project could be undertaken with much smaller hats. Straw hats are available in every conceivable size today, from tiny ones no more than 2 in (5 cm) in diameter to full-size adult ones.

POT POURRI FOR CHRISTMAS

There are a great many ways that pot pourri can come into its own for the Christmas holiday season. The evocative smells of this festival include those of pine needles, mulled wine, cinnamon and cranberries. There are several recipes in earlier chapters for Christmassy pot pourri but you may wish to think up one of your own instead.

Pot pourri around the crib
If you are planning to have a nativity scene either in your church or in your home, why not make a special hay/frankincense mix to sprinkle around the crib? This is a suggestion but you could adapt the ingredients to suit your stock of ingredients at the time.

Nativity pot pourri
1 cup red clover flowers
1 cup camomile flowers
1 cup small hop flowers
1 cup chopped violet leaves
1 cup jasmine flowers
1 cup orange flowers
1/4 cup crushed nutmeg
1/4 cup crushed cinnamon sticks

1/4 cup pieces of mace
1/4 cup star anise
1 cup cut calamus root or orris root
1 teaspoon violet oil
1 teaspoon frankincense oil
1/2 teaspoon myrrh oil
1/2 teaspoon patchouli oil

Soak the calamus or orris root with the oils. Leave for two days in a closed jam jar to mature. Then mix all the other ingredients and place in a polythene bag, sealed, for two weeks. Shake the mixture regularly during the two weeks and then check the fragrance. This can then be spread among the nativity figures and around the tableau.

Clove pomanders can be made from apples, oranges, lemons or limes, or an interesting mixture of all the citrus fruits. Allspice beads are another unusual gift to make for someone who shares your enthusiasm for subtle aromas!

SCENTED CHRISTMAS CARDS

Your Christmas cards could also be scented with very little trouble. Buy them a littler earlier than usual (well, earlier than I buy mine!), say in August or September, and take them all out of their wrapping if they have one. Then lay them in a large box with a well-fitting lid (with or without the envelopes depending on the space you have available), pack with them one or two of the highly scented sachets described in Chapter Seven and close the lid. Leave the cards for at least six weeks or more; when you come to write them they will be gently perfumed. It would be nice to create a Christmas smelling pot pourri for this job, or you could use a favourite floral or fruity mix instead.

This is a Christmas mix that proved very successful last time I made it.

Cranberry and orange celebration
1 cup strawberry leaves
1 cup orange peel
2 cups cut calamus root
1 teaspoon sweet orange oil
4 teaspoons cranberry oil
1 teaspoon cinnamon oil

Mix the calamus root with the oils and leave in a closed jam jar for two days to mature. Mix with the strawberry leaves and orange peel, place in a blender or grinder and reduce to a coarse powder. Store in a sealed polythene bag for a couple of weeks to mature, then use to fill sachets and place with the cards.

SCENTED WREATHS FOR CHRISTMAS

Although wreaths are beautiful all year round, they are especially popular at Christmas. They make a lovely welcoming feature on the front door or in any room in the house where you want to emphasize Christmas celebrations. Wreath bases can easily be bought from a craft supplier or florist, available in various twig or straw forms. Alternatively you could use a florists' foam ring for dried flower work. The convenience of a twig or straw wreath is that you can leave a portion uncovered and it adds to the design, whereas the foam-based rings must be completely covered.

Scented ivy wreaths
Collect as many lengths of ivy stems as you can, preferably over 5 ft (1.7 m) in length. Turn a stool or chair upside down and, using the legs as a guide, wrap the stems around in a circle. Tie with florists' wire occasionally to keep the ivy in shape and under control! When you are happy with the weight and shape, tie in the last strand and remove the wreath from the legs of the chair or stool.

While the wreath is drying, place it under a sheet of hardboard or something similar, and weigh the board down with anything in the cupboards that you can spare. Large (full) tins of baked beans are my usual method! Instead of ivy, you could use various plant stems, honeysuckle or grape vines, so experiment with whatever you have growing in your garden or nearby.

Once the wreath is dry you can begin to decorate it. I always use a hot-glue gun but you could wire the ingredients on to the wreath if you preferred. This is nothing like as easy and the wires are sometimes visible, from the back if not the front, so being a perfectionist I would choose the glue gun every time. These guns are not expensive and are easily purchased at any large DIY or hardware store. After you have bought one, your life will never be the same again! I have found a million things that I use it for and I've often wondered how we ever managed without one!

Ingredients to decorate the wreath

glycerined ivy leaves
small cinnamon sticks
ribbons
dried roses
glycerined clematis seed heads

small wooden balls or beads
essential oils
fabric
wires

Soak the wooden balls or beads in the essential oils for a few minutes, then remove them and leave to dry. Cut small circles, bigger than the balls, out of the fabric. Gather a fabric circle around each ball and fasten with a piece of wire.

Attach a selection of ivy leaves, either all the way round the wreath or just over a section of it depending on your chosen design. Then glue on the cinnamon sticks, tied in small bundles with gold cord. Add the clematis seed heads and dried roses. To attach the ribbon, make up a series of loops and wire them, then attach the wire or the base of the ribbon to the wreath.

Finally glue on the fabric-covered balls and double-check that all the ingredients have been securely attached. The wreath is now ready for hanging.

MAKING MINIATURE WREATHS

Although many wreaths are made in large sizes, say 12–18 in (30–45 cm) across, it can make a charming decoration to produce some smaller wreaths. Depending on the diameter that you choose, they can range from tiny rings to hang on Christmas trees to medium-sized rings that will hang on the wall. These instructions make a wreath that is slightly too large to hang on the tree but the measurements could easily be scaled down.

Ingredients

heavy gauge florists' wire (26–30 gauge)
oak moss or similar
ribbons

dried flowers and tiny cones scented
with oils

Using the base of a wine bottle as a guide, wrap the wire around it two or three times until you have a sturdy base for your wreath. Twist the end under or through the other wires to secure, and clip off the ends to tidy them. Wind the moss around the wreath, attaching it with a piece of finer wire here and there.

When you have a nicely mossed wreath base, you can begin the decoration. Again I would recommend using a glue gun rather than wire at this stage. Attach the scented cones and flowers in a design, either all around the ring or just covering half or two-thirds of it. Then glue on some loops or ribbon bows as a finishing touch.

FRAGRANT CHRISTMAS IDEAS

The idea of adding a little fragrance can be carried on through many traditional Christmas decorations. You could spray your tree with a mixture of seasonal smells, or buy a ready-mixed perfume oil in a suitable fragrance. One of the loveliest decorations at Christmas is a swag or garland of dried or fresh flowers and leaves, which can be hung across a mantelpiece, twined around the staircase or hung over a doorway.

Scented Christmas swag
boughs of blue spruce or other pine foliage
tartan ribbons
scented pine cones
small cinnamon sticks
gold cord
dried red roses and other flowers
tartan-covered scented wooden balls (see instructions for wreaths)
firm rope, ½–1 in (12–24 mm) in diameter, cut to the length required
large bundle of 24-gauge florists' wires, 7 in (17.5 cm) long

Take a piece of the 24-gauge (medium-weight) wire and bend it in half, opening it out a little into a loop, then wire it on to one end of the piece of rope to make a hanging loop. Repeat this on the other end. Cut the spruce into small pieces about 4–6 in (10–15 cm) long. Lay the first piece over the hanging loop at one end, to cover it, then bind the stem on to the rope with a piece of wire.

Cover the entire rope with pieces of spruce, wired on, until you have a green swag. Then either wire or glue on the tartan ribbons, made up into loops or bows. I would suggest placing one large bow in the middle of the swag and one at each end. If the swag is fairly long you can add loops or bows mid-way between the middle and the ends as well. The other ingredients can then be wired or glued into position. The tartan-covered

This apple and cinnamon wreath has had some extra drops of spicy oils dropped onto the base to add to the delicious smells.

balls can be grouped to look like tartan berries nestling among the foliage.

If you are going to hang this swag along a mantelpiece or anywhere near an open fire, then do take extra care when positioning it. Make sure that it is very firmly fixed and that there is no way that it could drop on to the hearth. It would only take one stray spark to start a very unwelcome bonfire.

Scented ornaments to hang on the tree

Making your own Christmas tree ornaments is a great family pastime as Christmas Day approaches. There is a selection of ideas here that will not only look attractive on the tree but will also give a festive perfume to the room.

Perfumed parcels

small blocks of balsa wood or other soft absorbent wood
essential oils
scraps of Christmas fabric
gold and silver cord or narrow ribbon

Soak the blocks of wood in a selection of essential oils. Some of the parcels could be cinnamon, some sweet orange, others cranberry, pine needle or perhaps eucalyptus. Choosing the scents is part of the fun!

Remove the wood from the oil and allow it to dry out. Then wrap the blocks in pieces of Christmas material, gluing the ends of the parcels rather than using sticky tape. Tie round the pieces of cord or ribbon. Add a hanging loop at the centre top of the parcel so that it hangs straight on the tree.

Scented pottery hearts

small amount of clay or modelling dough
essential oils
sharp implement to make holes for ribbon
narrow ribbons

Roll out the clay like pastry and, using a heart-shaped cutter or any other suitable shape (holly leaves or Christmas trees perhaps), cut out a number of ornaments. Using a sharp knitting needle or similar, make a hole in the top of each shape to thread the ribbon through later.

Soak the clay shapes in the essential oils and then leave to dry or bake in a very cool oven. Thread the ribbons through the holes you made earlier and hang the hearts from the tree.

Other ideas

Sachets shaped like Christmas stockings could be filled with a strongly scented pot pourri. The scented wooden balls can be made into little figures or even Christmas puddings. Bundles of cinnamon sticks can be decorated with scented cones. There are many possibilities once you have started on the scented trail, but beware of getting to the stage where anything that doesn't move gets soaked in essential oils – it can happen!

SUMMER SCENTS ALL YEAR ROUND

Christmas is not the only time of year when we want our houses to smell delicious. The fragrance of summer flowers is with us for such a short time that it is lovely to be able to prolong the smells of that season by using pot pourri and other scented items throughout the house. Here are a few ideas that will capture that fleeting fragrance and keep it for ages.

Fragrant photos

Photographs are memories, and whether they are in individual frames or in an album, there are ways to add fragrance to them that can increase their significance. If you have a treasured wedding album you could make up strong sachets of powdered pot pourri using perfumes connected with the wedding. If you carried lily of the valley, gardenias or roses on your wedding day then make a floral pot pourri bouquet and barely fill small sachets with it. Place these flat sachets between the pages at each end of the album, or in the box it is kept in, and the smell of flowers will prevade the whole book. Do not place the sachet directly next to a photograph in case it is damaged by the essential oils.

The same idea can be applied to family albums. Pick a scent that reminds you of a certain holiday or celebration and tuck it into the album or box, then when you look through the pictures, the perfume will strengthen your memory. You could choose a festive pot pourri mix for Christmas memories, a fruit-based recipe to remind you of a children's party (orange jelly with vanilla custard, perhaps?) Memories of a trip to the mountains could be rekindled with a mix of pine and herbs. Think back to the fragrances that are part of the memory and see if you can encapsulate them into a pot pourri mix.

If the photograph you want to perfume is displayed in an individual frame, then there are two possibilities. If it is in a particularly lovely frame, then simply attach a small strongly scented sachet to the back of the frame. However, if you either have a rather dull frame that could do with cheering up or no frame at all then this idea might just suit.

Decorated photoframe

Use a wooden frame and place the photograph inside it. It is important to work with the photograph in place as the flowers will overlap the photo and it looks very odd if a rose-bud covers the face of one of the people in a group shot!

Using a glue gun again, attach some leaves or ferns to the bottom left-hand corner of the frame. This acts as a base on which to build up your design using dried roses, statice or *Helichrysum*, for example. The flowers or leaves should overlap the photograph slightly to soften the edges, but not so much as to obscure the contents of the photograph. Make sure there are plenty of dainty ingredients such as gypsophila or herb sprigs to soften the arrangement. A few large flowers stuck on to the frame do not give such a pretty effect.

When you are happy with your design, add some drops of essential oil to all the main ingredients; your frame will look lovely and smell delicious. You don't have to decorate the bottom left-hand corner only – you could go all around the frame, or add flowers top right to balance the bottom left group. If you enjoy making this, you could decorate several frames and create a different design for each one.

Other scented objects and ornaments
A scented sachet can also be used to scent notepaper, cards or your favourite books. A special hat box makes a wonderful place to keep treasured mementoes and you could add a strongly scented sachet with these memories incorporated into the mixture.

Small flower arrangements always look attractive in bedrooms and bathrooms, and while searching for a suitable container I came upon some medium sized and large shells. These can be grouped together or displayed individually. The larger ones I used to hold pot pourri and the smaller ones were filled with dry florists' foam, then groups of rose-buds, pearls and ribbons were placed into the foam. You can then paint the shell with essential oil and add a few drops to the dried flowers.

Pot pourri can also be used to cover polystyrene or ceramic shapes, which gives a very unusual effect. Tiny polystyrene balls could be covered to make tree ornaments or tiny pomanders, or you could attempt a larger project as described below.

Fragrant lavender bear
1 small to medium ceramic teddy bear (several companies manufacture money boxes in this shape)
large pot of latex adhesive
quantity of lavender
narrow lavender ribbon
3 dried rose-buds
small bottle of lavender essential oil

Coat the teddy figure with the glue, watering it down slightly if it seems to be too thick. Then sit the gluey bear on an upturned cup and heap the lavender evenly all over him. Pat the lavender down firmly and make sure there is an even coating or you will have a balding bear! Then leave the bear to dry overnight.

When the bear is dry and you are happy that he is evenly covered (you can always stick a few more bits and pieces on if there is a thin patch), glue on a ribbon around his neck and a cluster of rose-buds in his paw. Finally, add some drops of lavender oil to increase the natural perfume of the lavender flowers.

Favourite pictures and photographs can be fragranced by rubbing essential oils into the wood at the back of the frame, or by decorating them with dried flowers and then dropping a small amount of oil onto the flowers.

Suppliers

Miscellaneous

Joanna Sheen Ltd
P.O. Box 52
Newton Abbot
Devon
TQ12 4YF
England
Tel: (0626) 872405 (mail order and enquiries accepted worldwide)
(retail and wholesale, most items used in the book)

Essential Oils

Essential oils are also available from many health food shops and other
pot pourri stockists

Index

Page numbers in *italics* refer to the illustrations

INDEX